RURAL ARCHITECTURE
of the American Southwest

RURAL ARCHITECTURE
of the American Southwest
Featuring Fences, Barns and Corrals

MYRTLE STEDMAN

SUNSTONE PRESS

SANTA FE

Copyright © 1989 by Myrtle Stedman

All Rights Reserved.
No part of this book may be reproduced in any form or by any
electronic or mechanical means including information storage and
retrieval systems, without permission in writing from the publisher,
except by a reviewer who may quote brief passages in a review.

Printed in the United States of America

Library of Congress Cataloging in Publication Data:

Stedman, Myrtle
  Rural architecture of northern New Mexico and southern Colorado : featuring fences, barns, and corrals / Myrtle Stedman.
      p.   cm.
   Bibliography: p.
   1. Fences — New Mexico. 2. Barns — New Mexico. 3. Corrals — New Mexico. 4. Fences — Colorado. 5. Barns — Colorado. 6. Corrals — Colorado. I. Title.
NA8301.S74   1989
ISBN: 0-86534-001-3
728'.92'097883–dc19   88-30116
                                                                                CIP

WWW.SUNSTONEPRESS.COM
SUNSTONE PRESS / POST OFFICE BOX 2321 / SANTA FE, NM 87504-2321 /USA
(505) 988-4418 / ORDERS ONLY (800) 243-5644 / FAX (505) 988-1025

DEDICATED TO —
   Anya, Austin, Clasien,
   Christina, Michelle, Christopher
   and the one now on the way to be born.

Foreword

I am pleased that Myrtle Stedman asked me to write a foreword for her new book *Rural Architecture of Northern New Mexico and Southern Colorado*. The occasion provides me a welcome opportunity to comment, not only upon the merits of the present work, but also upon the considerable contribution of the author in the field of native Southwestern architecture.

During the 1950s and 1960s, the use of local building styles and traditional materials seemed to be on the wane in northern New Mexico. I recall architects telling me that adobe construction was uneconomical and that it would soon be entirely displaced by new high tech products then coming on the market. The few individuals, moved by a romantic view of the past, who were still building with unfired earth bricks, pine roof beams, and juniper or aspen ceiling poles would be gone by the next generation, they said.

But then, lo, something happened! The historic architecture of the Southwest rapidly began to win a new popularity. The turnaround, I suppose, was partly a product of the back-to-earth movement, the energy crises of the 1970s, and a reawakening of interest in regional history. But it received a boost, too, from advances in the use of solar energy—many of the new developments being especially adaptable to adobe structures. Individuals planning their dream house led the way, but many home builders and architects, taking note of the demand, followed the trend setters.

At the same time, "how-to" books and articles on New Mexico's traditional architecture began to find a large readership. There was even a handsome periodical for devotees, *Adobe News*, each issue replete with advice, information, and the advertisements of contractors and sellers of adobe products. The renaissance, for such it should be termed, had been properly launched.

Among those in the forefront of this small phenomenon was artist and writer Myrtle Stedman. A long-time resident of the Santa Fe area, she had been a champion of the old ways in building for much of her adult life. Indeed, her books *Adobe Architecture* and *Adobe Remodeling and Fireplaces* in significant measure helped spark the return to traditional construction.

Now Mrs. Stedman has added to her earlier accomplishments with the present sketchbook, focusing on the numerous fascinating and picturesque aspects of rural architecture in northern New Mexico and southern Colorado. Her splendid pen and ink drawings, reminding one of Eric Sloane's work on rural America, have a three-fold value.

In the first instance, they serve as an accurate documentary record of features and styles that comprise the unique architecture of this area. Secondly, the drawings will prove a boon to those wishing to restore buildings and improve rural properties along traditional lines. And finally, the artistic merit and natural charm of the sketchbook should appeal to all those who possess an aesthetic appreciation for the Southwestern landscape, be it natural or that part which is manmade.

That corner of our country watered by the upper Rio Grande has long provided a congenial cradle for the nurturing of creative, independent-minded, thoughtful, and sensitive persons. Myrtle Stedman, as one of the daughters of this land, has made a lasting contribution toward preserving what is here worthwhile and beautiful.

—Marc Simmons
Los Cerrillos, New Mexico

Preface

There are three cultures in the area this book covers: Native American, Spanish, and Anglo. All three have had their effect on the rural architecture of the land. The Indian type, according to Oliver LaFarge, has been here for over 20,000 years. These earliest settlers and their descendants, the Pueblo Indians, were and are skilled to an amazing degree in using timbers and stones, the mountain cliffs, the sun and the earth. Isolated from other people but close to the elements, they developed a science and an architecture so fitting to the landscape and climate that we are still emulating them. Centuries ago they were using solar energy by building on the ledges of cliffs under overhanging rocks which shielded them from the high riding summer sun—and in winter when the sun's angle reached in under the cliffs, their massive adobe walls absorbed the heat and radiated it into the interiors on cold days and nights. Where they built on the mesas, they turned their backs to the prevailing winds and cupped the sun with D or U-shaped buildings.

They had few domesticated animals until the Spanish came. When they had the land to themselves, they had no need to shelter or corral. When they did find this necessary, they developed a system of barns and corrals apart from or within their pueblos; if apart, not far away, and here all the animals were kept together. Today, only dogs are allowed to roam free in the pueblo. In the early days, writers noted that some of the Indian villages were palisaded for protection from other roving Indians by logs set upright and close together in the ground with the tops pointed and sharp. Some of these fences are still to be seen—although their purpose has obviously changed.

When the Spanish came up through Old Mexico (1610-1821) looking for gold (which they never found) and then for Indian souls to win to the Church and the crown of Spain, they brought animals, and settlers with iron tools and more highly developed skills—but there were no building materials in their mule and wagon trains.

Timber was plentiful in the Sangre de Cristos, San Juan, and Manzano ranges, and underfoot was an earth suitable for making sun-dried *adobe* bricks or for plastering. All of the homes and outbuildings of both the Indians and the Spanish-Americans were *principally* of these two materials or a combination of them; with stone. The Indians cut rounded logs with stone hatchets. The Spanish-Americans with their iron axes cut and dressed logs on two sides, leaving the top and bottom round. Both cultures chinked between the logs with adobe and both very often plastered the whole building with mud. It is not always apparent what was under the plaster, but where the plaster has been washed away it is very often seen to be logs. There is probably the greatest concentration of folk log structures in this area extant in the United States, although the New Mexico variety is distinctly different from Eastern log cabins in the way they vary in form and function. There is a preference for doors to be located on the long side rather than the gable end; the saddle notch is employed, but not the dovetail, half dovetail, or the square notch. And constantly we see that the functional design is shaped by the land and what it has to offer to the imagination and ingenuity.

One of the oldest varieties of log buildings was the jacal (upright logs set into the ground and plastered over). Marc Simmons, in his *New Mexico: A History*, writes of the private houses called jacales and Paul Horgan, in *The Centuries of Santa Fe*, writes of the old parish church which was at the east end of the Santa Fe plaza as "rather like a large jacal." Later this type of building was used only for outbuildings, except on such rare occasions as the one of which I write on page 36.

Spain lost its hold on the land through the independence of Mexico, and in 1846 the area became a territory of the United States. The early Spanish-Americans had ventured north into what is now Colorado. The boundary of New Mexico Territory moved south, but the results of the Spanish-American stay in southern Colorado remained.

However, by this time the wagon trains and traders were coming in from Kansas and points farther east, bringing such materials as galvanized iron and window glass. Among the new settlers were people from Germany and Finland. And, wherever people were close to the trade routes—even by train—pitched roofs which had been board and batten became dressed with metal. The Yankee or Anglo-American brought himself and everything with him, but all things of good taste fit in, the birthright belonging then, as it does largely today, to the American Indians and the Spanish-Americans.

The rural architecture of this area is distinctly native to this land. The artist, the rancher, and the builder in me made me want to do this in-the-field sketchbook on fences, barns, and corrals of northern New Mexico and southern Colorado. I have been living in the country, admiring these structures, and inwardly crying whenever I see one in disuse and in need of repair, or already in a state of ruin. This is my way of preserving them as they are today. The ones in use will remain in use and the ones in ruin will not fall down. Actually, I am heartened to see a trend in young people to reconstruct and to learn from past methods of building with local and at-hand materials such as adobe and the native timbers. I am grateful, too, to note the trend to make things beautiful while one is at the same time doing something practical and functional. The word simplicity, in my mind, covers this attitude. It in no way describes an imbecilic or artsy approach, but one of grace and economy, doing something to serve a purpose.

I find more people wanting a cow, a goat, some chickens and maybe a sow. I find especially that there are more people keeping saddle and even show horses today. If one doesn't have or want animals there is always a need for a place to store wood, bicycles, garden equipment, extra furniture. Or maybe there is just a need to have a place to rest in an appropriately designed shade area for which these sketches may provide a source of inspiration.

I am happy to see more palisade fences being constructed for privacy and design. The small fir, cedar or aspen limbs (latias) placed upright and close together have always proved a deterrent to coyotes snitching sheep. For a long time I only knew them as "coyote" fences. They are also known in Spanish as "circos de latia." For my latia fences I obtain a permit from the U.S. Forest Service to go up after fallen aspen poles. By using these fallen aspens, I feel I am helping clean up a potential fire hazard rather than depleting a natural resource. These fences and the use of native shrubs which grow of their own accord help to blend one's property into the natural surroundings rather than having one's whole place look like a transplant from some other part of the country, as some do. A great many of us are transplants, "not from here," but we have come to join in our surroundings and not change anything particularly.

Some of these barns are transplants which, I feel, have gracefully settled in and become a worthwhile part of the overall picture. Some are more recently built, utilizing advanced ideas and materials. One is a modern solar barn which depicts the new look on the horizon and, strangely enough, is in one of our oldest mountain villages of New Mexico. Barns and fences should match the style of the house one lives in and usually do.

The only reason for showing some houses in this book is to illustrate this point. I wanted to stress the shelters which are so typically native and which, I am told by horse owners, are more practical than stables and the animals prefer them. In the first place, they breathe. They are easier to clean and they fit into the landscape. The hay, which is usually stored on the flat roof, is handy to fork down to the mangers; it is safe from being devoured by roving animals and safe from ground rot. The hay acts as roof insulation. It keeps the sun off the shelter, and in the winter keeps animal body heat in. The latia walls are reinforced for wind and winter protection by piñon, cedar, and fir branches stacked against them, and are delightful to see. At the same time, they tell you something about the owner.

There is a uniqueness here found nowhere else in the United States. This is a land of mesas, mountain ranges, a few rivers, and watercourses called arroyos in which water floods violently after a rain—tumbling uprooted trees and old or new cars (with or without occupants) in its path—but in a few hours are dry again. There are vast desert lands under blazing sun and in the winter fierce, cutting, and icy winds and driving snow—but the snow, too, soon disappears. Even in the desert areas there are piñon, spruce, and fir, sagebrush and chamisa—all below clear blue skies or dramatic storm clouds. One can sometimes see three separate rainstorms in the same direction.

I hope this will be an idea book, a "how-to-do-it" book, or one which will give you a chance to use your ingenuity—or at least help you share an appreciation of our rural architecture of northern New Mexico and southern Colorado. The Old World look is becoming frail and fragile, but it so befits the land that I hope we can retain and utilize more of its ways and beauty.

There are miles of these fences in Nambe and in other communties of northern New Mexico and southern Colorado.

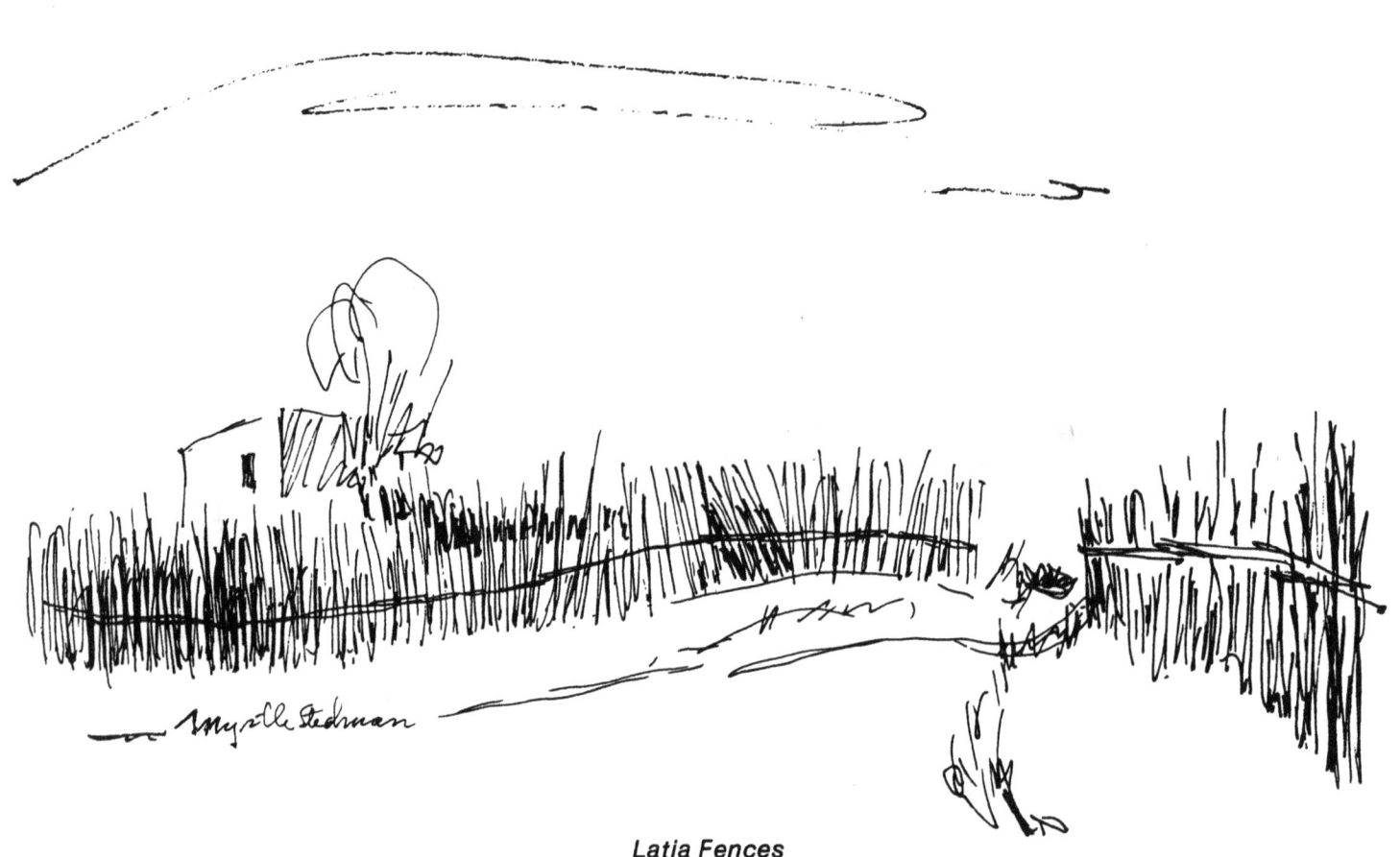

Latia Fences

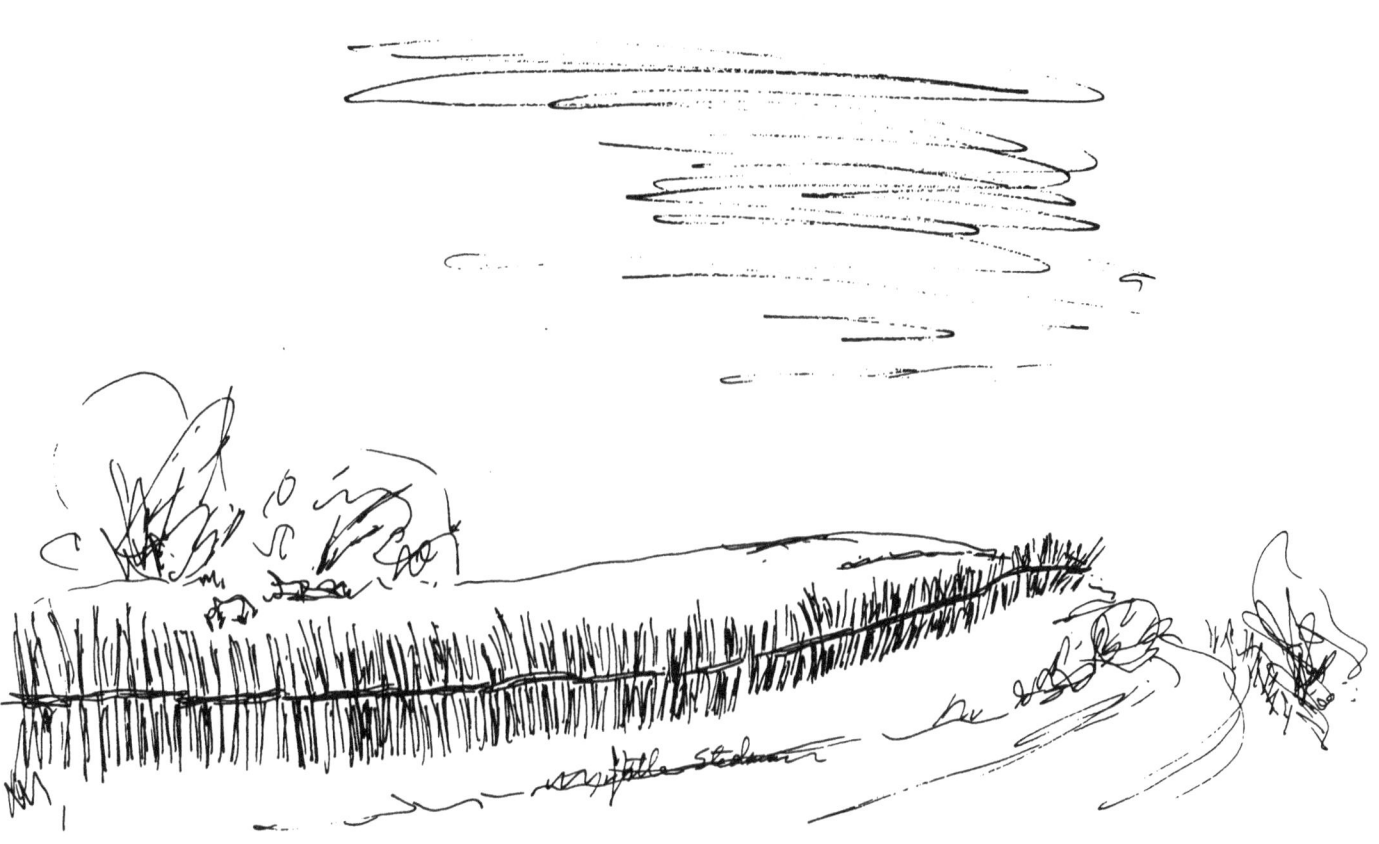

This fence has only one rail. The latias (poles) were set into a shallow trench, then the dirt was kicked up against them to hold them in place.

Latia Fence

An Anglo American Home In Tesuque

Latia, or latilla, is the diminutive of the word lata, which means a small piece of wood. Latia fences are as prominent an architectural feature of our landscape as adobe houses. Nothing in a community or city does a better job of tying us into our rural or local atmosphere than a latia fence.

Four Ways to Build a Latia Fence: All latia fences have to be built on a skeleton structure of good strong cedar posts, their butts planted into the ground to below frost-line depth, spaced six to eight feet apart, with some sort of connection between them for fastening the latias.

In drawing #1 you can see this illustrated by rails wired to the posts with double strands of wire. The rails are longer than the distance between the posts, and overlap each other at the post. The latias in this drawing are then stood up on the ground and wired to the top rail first, one at a time in an under-through-and over-the-rail motion of the wire. Baling wire saved from bales of hay is most commonly used, but construction wire obtained from lumber yards accomplishes the same thing. The wire is flexible enough to be handled easily in pieces cut six or eight feet long. It takes two people to put the fence together—one person on either side of the fence to grasp the wire as it is passed through from side to side and to pull it up tightly, drawing the latias snugly against the rail.

When one length of wire is used up, another can be attached to its end by a loop-in-loop joint with the ends going in opposite directions. Unless the ends of the wires turn back from the interlocking loop, the connection may slip and let the fence come apart at that place.

These fences are heavy and should be strongly built. The rails can be aspen, slender elm or locust, pine, or whatever is available. If they are dry, they are lighter and less apt to sag or twist. The main thing is to get the cedar posts in solidly and not too far apart.

Drawing #2 shows the latias more or less plaited between two strands of wire, top and bottom.

Drawing #3 shows them wired to two strands of an existing barbed wire fence.

Drawing #4 shows a continuous series of cedar posts set in the ground and wired to horizontal rails, beginning like fence #1. This is the king of them all, but it hurts me to think of its price and extravagant use of resources. My fallen-aspen-pole fences have lasted for over forty years and are still in good shape. I don't want to encourage people to strip our hillsides for miles around, even though I love these cedar pole fences dearly.

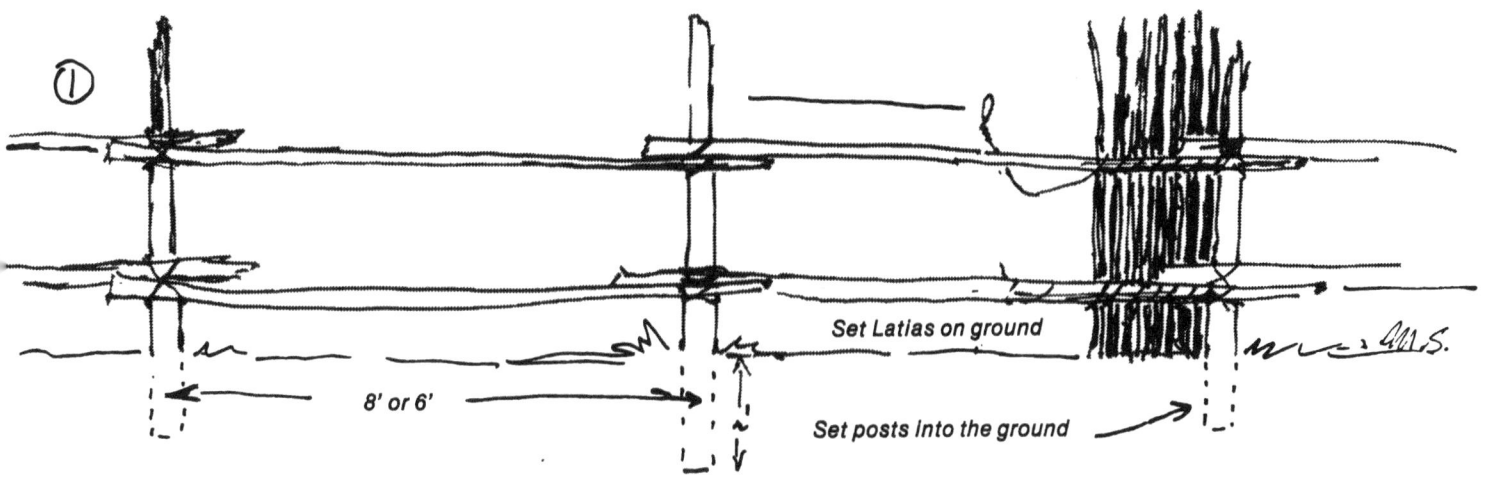

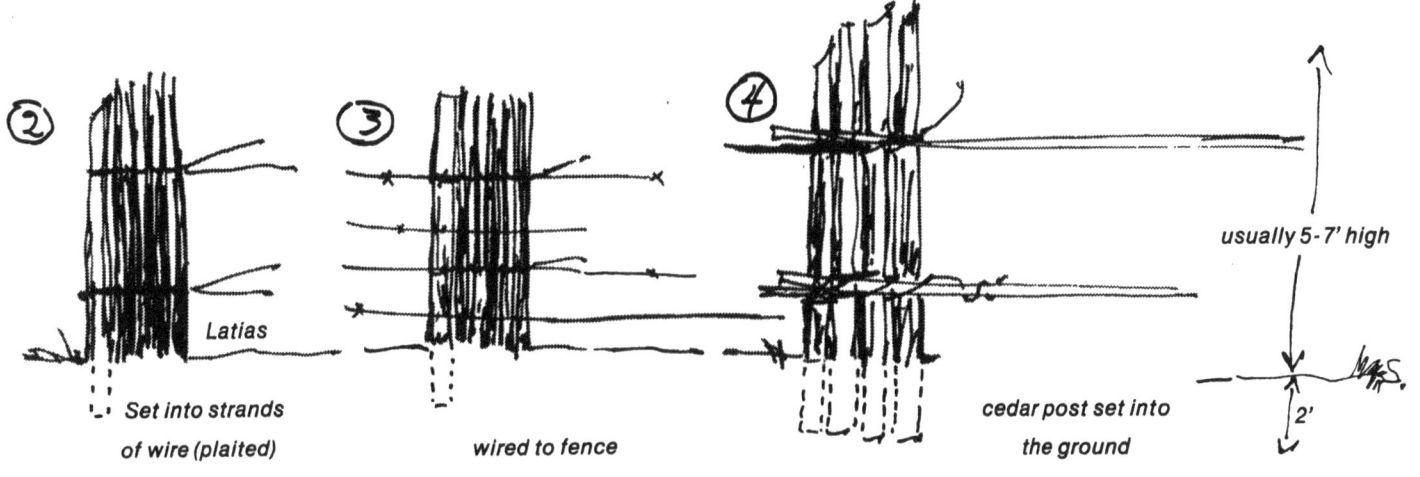

The Loggia

At the Taos Pueblo

Many of our architectural forms in this area were designed by the Indians and adapted for use by Spanish-Americans and Anglos alike because they were so logical. This chain of loggias in Taos Pueblo is a classic example. You can see in it the basic design for horse shelters, woodsheds, and all kinds of outdoor shelters. Here, in its simplest form, it is free-standing in the plaza, creating shade for selling pottery and jewelry, hanging blankets and wares or storing wood. It is simply huge cedar or juniper posts set deeply into the ground with forks at their tops which hold cross-beams over which lie latias placed closely together to give the structure its platform roof.

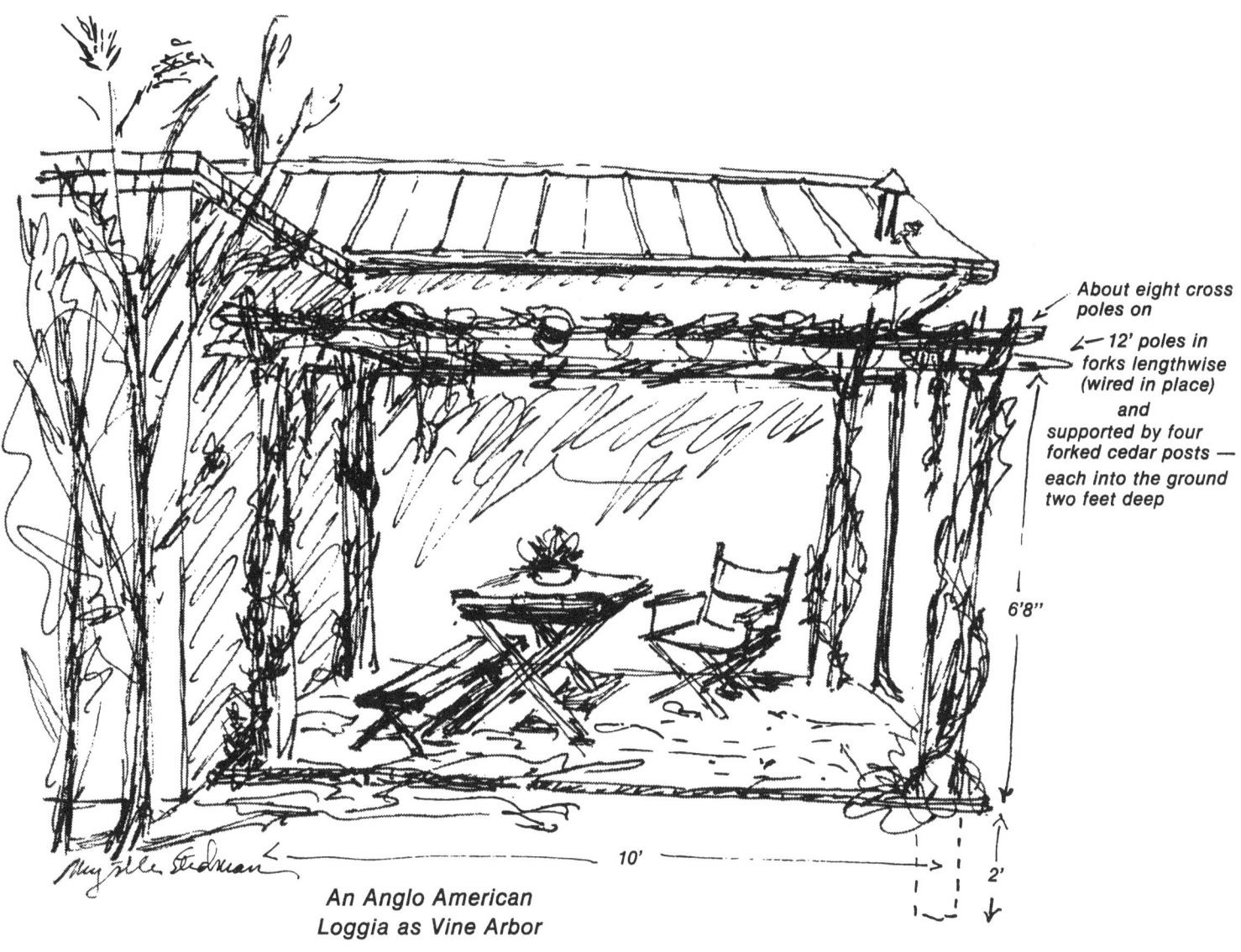

An Anglo American Loggia as Vine Arbor

Road

This double-page spread is of buildings on a land grant made by the King of Spain to Cristobal de la Serna. (He happened to be in El Paso during the 1680 Pueblo Revolt against the Spanish.) The grant covered hundreds and hundreds of acres, taking in Ranchos de Taos, Quemado, and Cordillera. The grant is still known by Serna's name, though it has been divided many times. These buildings are on a small portion in Cordillera.

The area came by its name when this house was one of seven large houses (haciendas with walls around them) like seven mountains (cordilleras) in a row on the horizon along the back road from Ranchos de Taos to Taos.

The same family owned this house for years, and it grew lengthwise and into side wings with each new generation. A single member of the family was living in this lovely old adobe when I drew the sketch. Originally there were four rooms. At present there are seven, but the occupant remembers when there were seventeen rooms and her sister remembers when there were more, the largest a sala.

Ranchos de Taos Carport

The log cabin (fuerte) was the family storage place for fruits and potatoes. There was once a dispensa, a smoke house, a huge wood pile and stables, even a winery at the bottom of the hill, she told me. There was no garage; the car sat in this area in the sun. I suggested the logia carport. The lady, however, built a double garage at the other end of the place, but was horrified at the cost — money that she'd intended to put into the remodeling of the house.

Circa 1890 Spanish American

Again and again you can see posts sunk into the ground to support roof structures, and you sometimes find that the walls are nothing more than these latia fences. This is a Spanish-American barn, identifiable by its peaked roof. The Spanish name for the peaked-roof barn is *tasolera*—originally Mexican *tlazol* or *clasol* (see "Human Geography of the Southwest" in *Landscape*, Winter 1952, Vol. I, no. 3, pp. 31-2).

In Cerro — A Horse Barn and Corral, "Estable"

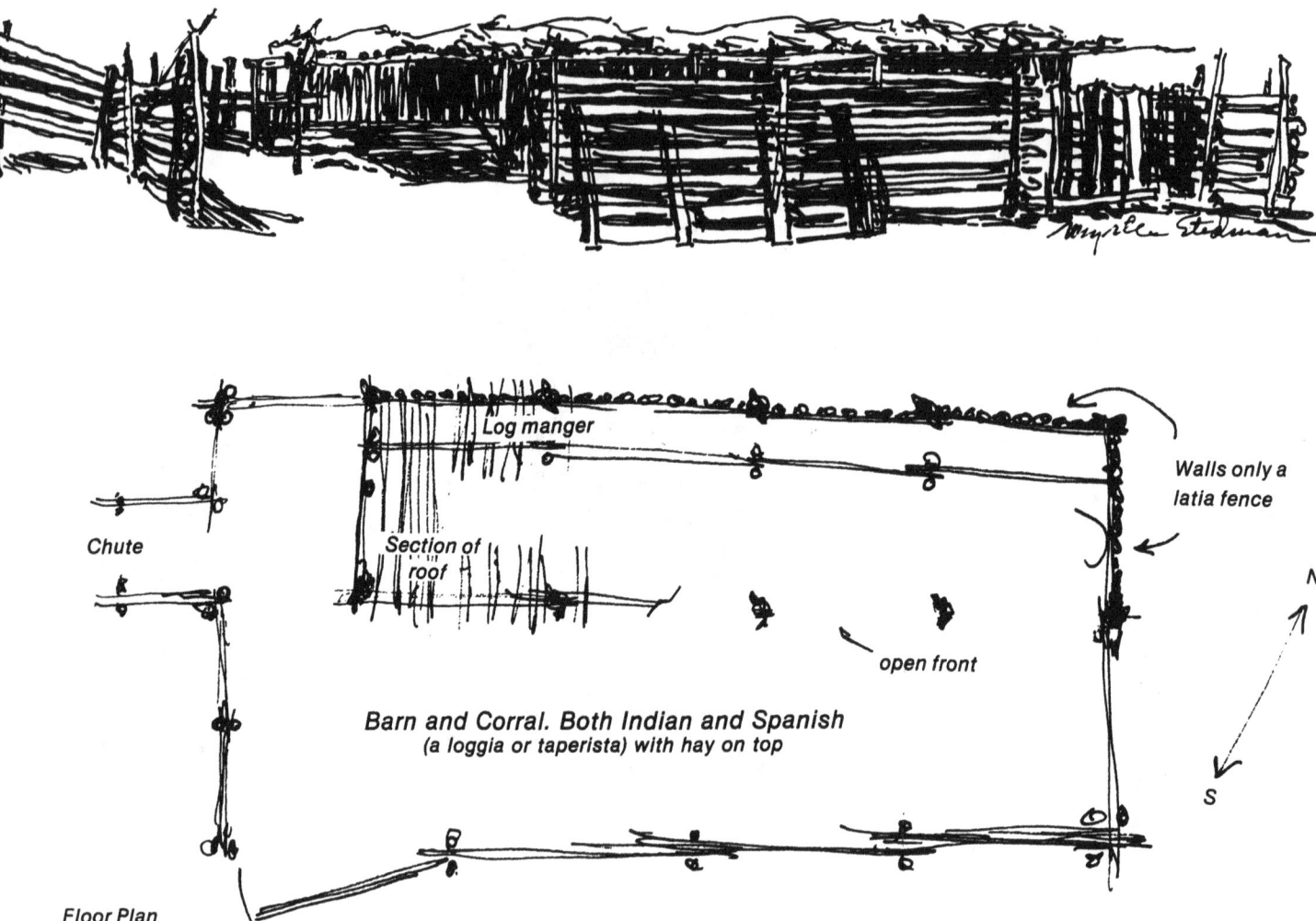

Roybal's at Cuyamungue

The people who owned this barn were pleased that I was drawing it, and invited me into the house to show "Mama." Mama gave me a cup of coffee, then a piece of cake, and in a few minutes some delicious jam to go with it. The family was more than willing to eagerly tell me about "Papa," who built the barn. I promised them an autographed copy of the book. Then they took me to a neighbor who had a nice barn, and he too was delightful. He showed me his woodworking shop where he made things to "kill time." His place was immaculate and he asked me to come visit anytime.

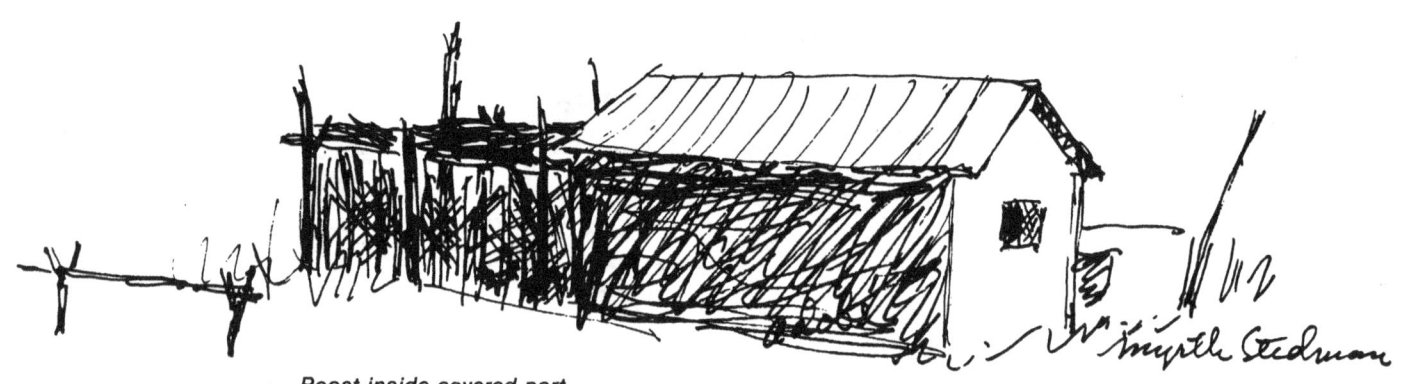

The Roybal's adobe chicken house and covered run

Roost inside covered part

 Apple box nests

Anglo American or Spanish American

Root Cellars, area of Fort Garland

These trees provide shade for a large pasture. A smaller variety, the bush or brook willow, was many years ago an indispensable building material. Its branches and leaves were used over ceiling and roof decks of latias—to reinforce mud and several inches of dirt on flat roofs and woven into jacal walls to help hold mud plaster.

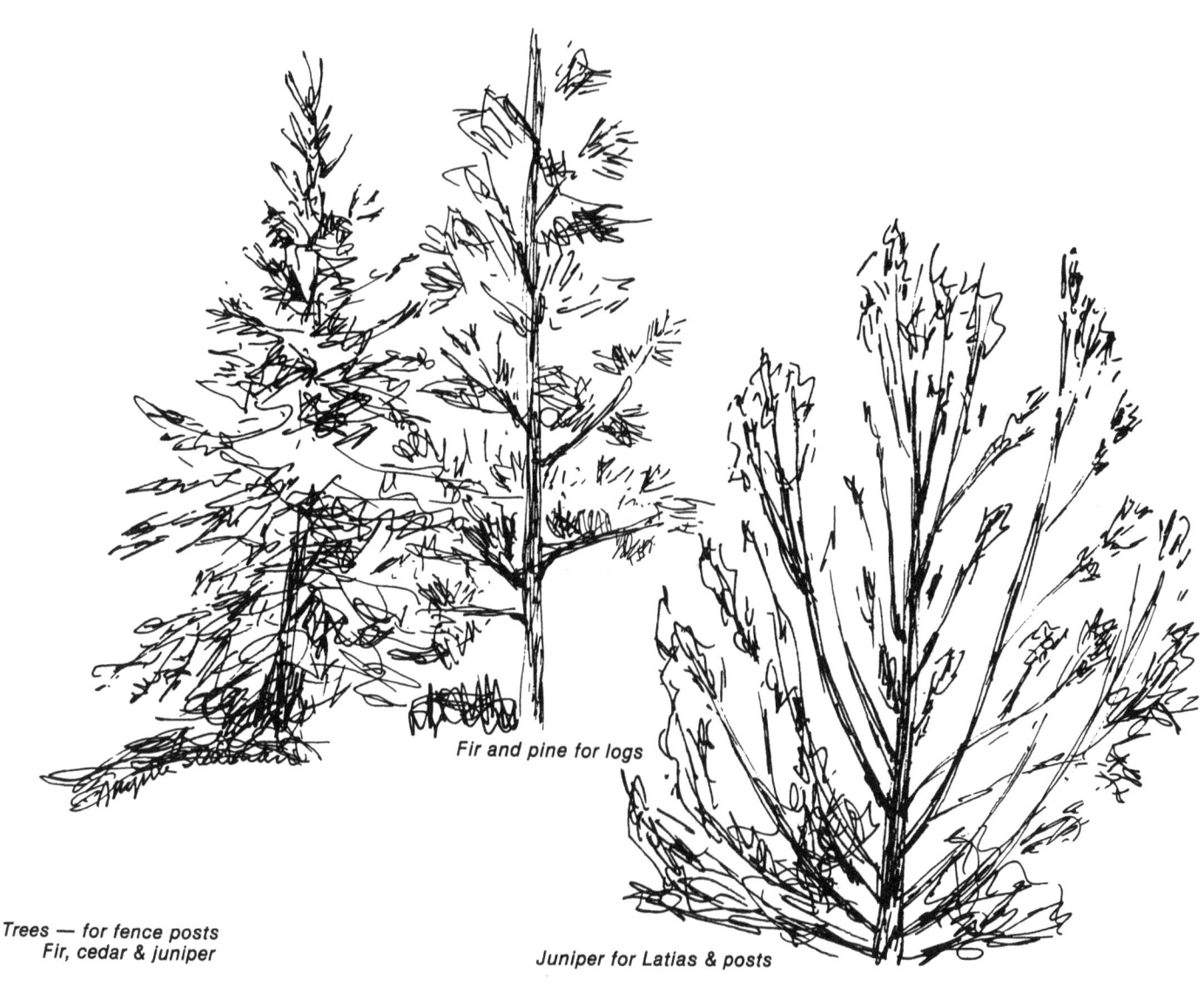

Trees — for fence posts
Fir, cedar & juniper

Fir and pine for logs

Juniper for Latias & posts

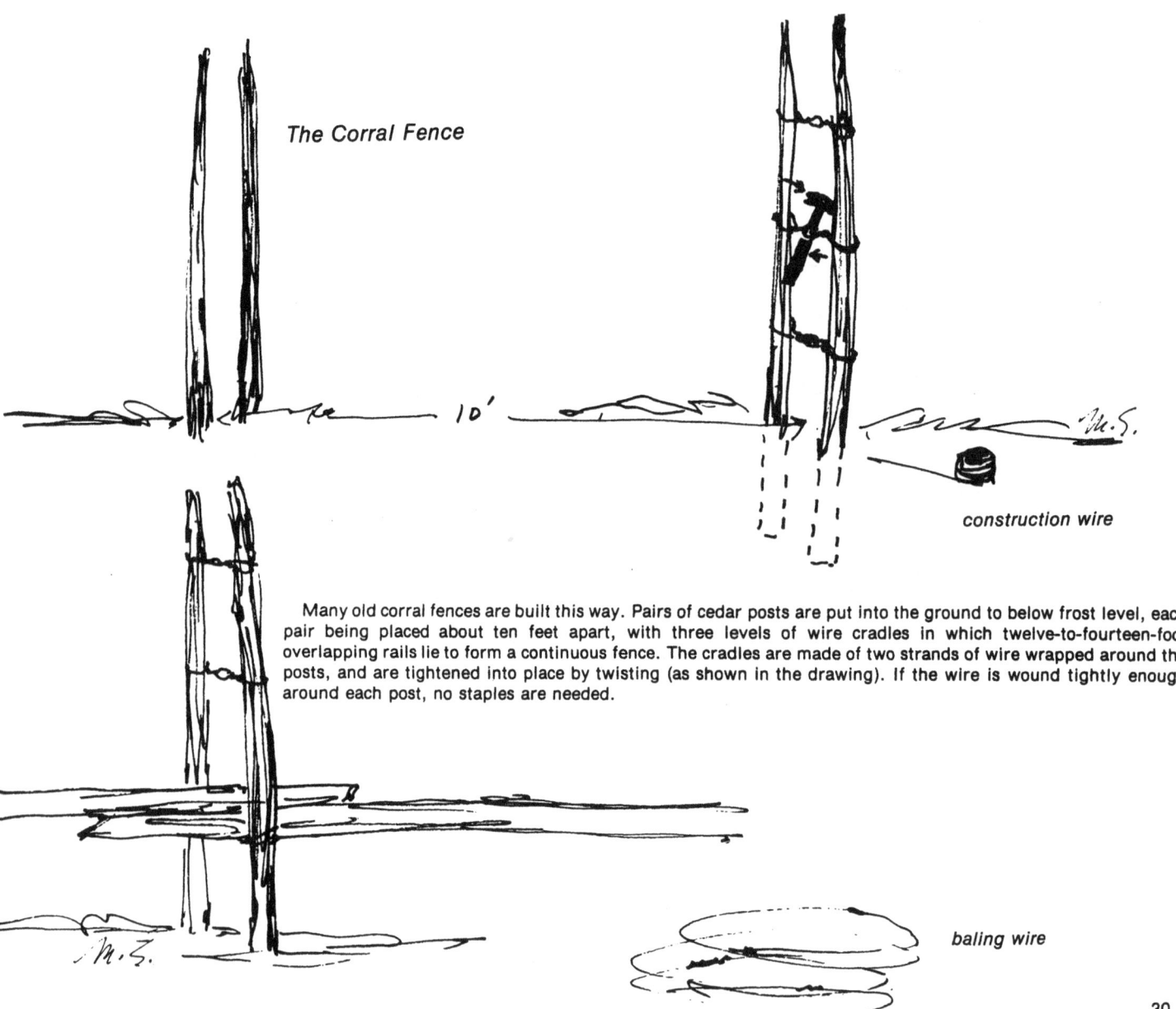

The Corral Fence

construction wire

Many old corral fences are built this way. Pairs of cedar posts are put into the ground to below frost level, each pair being placed about ten feet apart, with three levels of wire cradles in which twelve-to-fourteen-foot overlapping rails lie to form a continuous fence. The cradles are made of two strands of wire wrapped around the posts, and are tightened into place by twisting (as shown in the drawing). If the wire is wound tightly enough around each post, no staples are needed.

baling wire

Horse barn and corral

These corrals, once very important, are practically deserted today.

*Squared log feed and tack rooms
and horse shelter at Taos Pueblo*

*In the Santa Cruz area —
Spanish American*

This complex was very much in use when I sketched it. The horses just happened to be gone, either in a pasture or on a jaunt with riders.

At Taos Pueblo outdoor log manger and barn.

Spanish American

Jacal and Fuerte: Something really tugged at my heart when I walked through this jacal and fuerte house (on the following page), as though I might have had humble beginnings in such a place. There certainly was a feeling of coziness about it—two rooms to live in, a large animal room, and a hallway. It was actually built as two free-standing log cabins with a space between them and a single roof over all. Later, the space between the cabins was closed in to form the hallway or zaguan, as it is called. The whole structure thus created was once chinked and plastered with mud and clay, and looked like one all-adobe house with a peaked roof. In the loft, there was hay to preserve the warmth of the house and feed the animals.

Jacal (ha-'cal) and fuerte (fu-air-tay) are Old World terms transported to the New World, and are still found in Old Mexico and southern New Mexico. Jacal means walls made of vertical poles or sticks, chinked and plastered with mud or clay; and fuerte means fort or fortification. The jacal parts of this house are the two outside walls of the hallway, which have doorways in them. The fuerte parts are the two log cabins on either side of that hallway.

You can tell that the header beams and the girders for the jacal walls were built in as the log fuerte construction was going up because they are locked in place, bottom and top, by notched logs from front to back that are a part of the log cabins. The headers are round logs, groved in the underside so that the jacal material (which, in this case, was slabs—the sawmill's first trim from dressing logs- still with the bark on them) could be stood up into the groove and rested on the girder. They were fixed in place to girders by baseboards.

I know of one nice Anglo-American home recently constructed in all-jacal manner. The walls are of sturdy cedar posts treated and set into a trench, with the earth then packed back against them and the ground sloping away for good drainage. The posts are leveled off at the top and a wall plate carries a flat roof. Its floors are mud and the walls, inside and out, are chinked and plastered with mud. This is a beautiful and very sophisticated small house. I am not sure how many building codes it meets or breaks. To all outward appearances, it looks like an adobe. On page 38 you will see a jacal and fuerte ruin and some detailed drawings of construction.

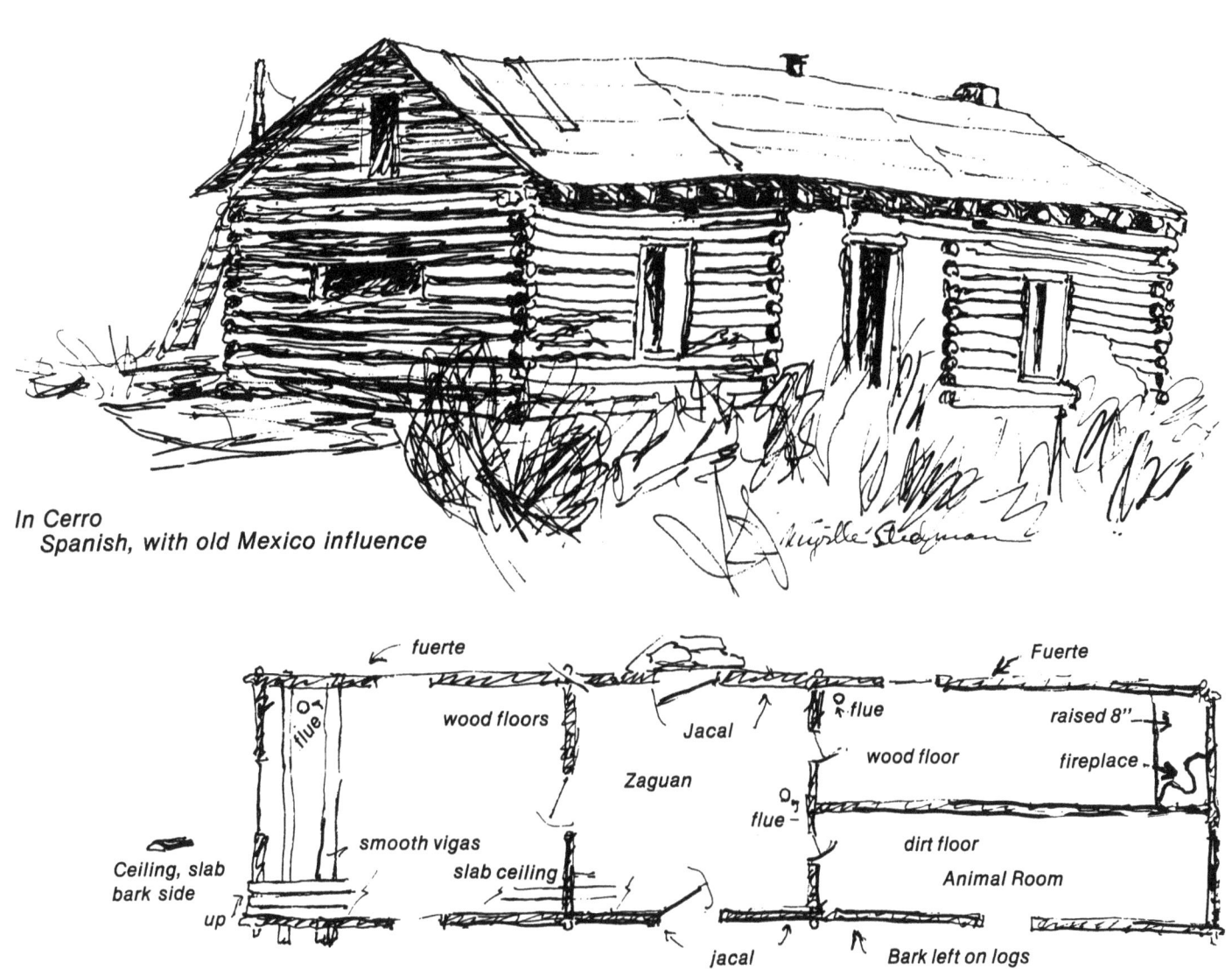

In Cerro
Spanish, with old Mexico influence

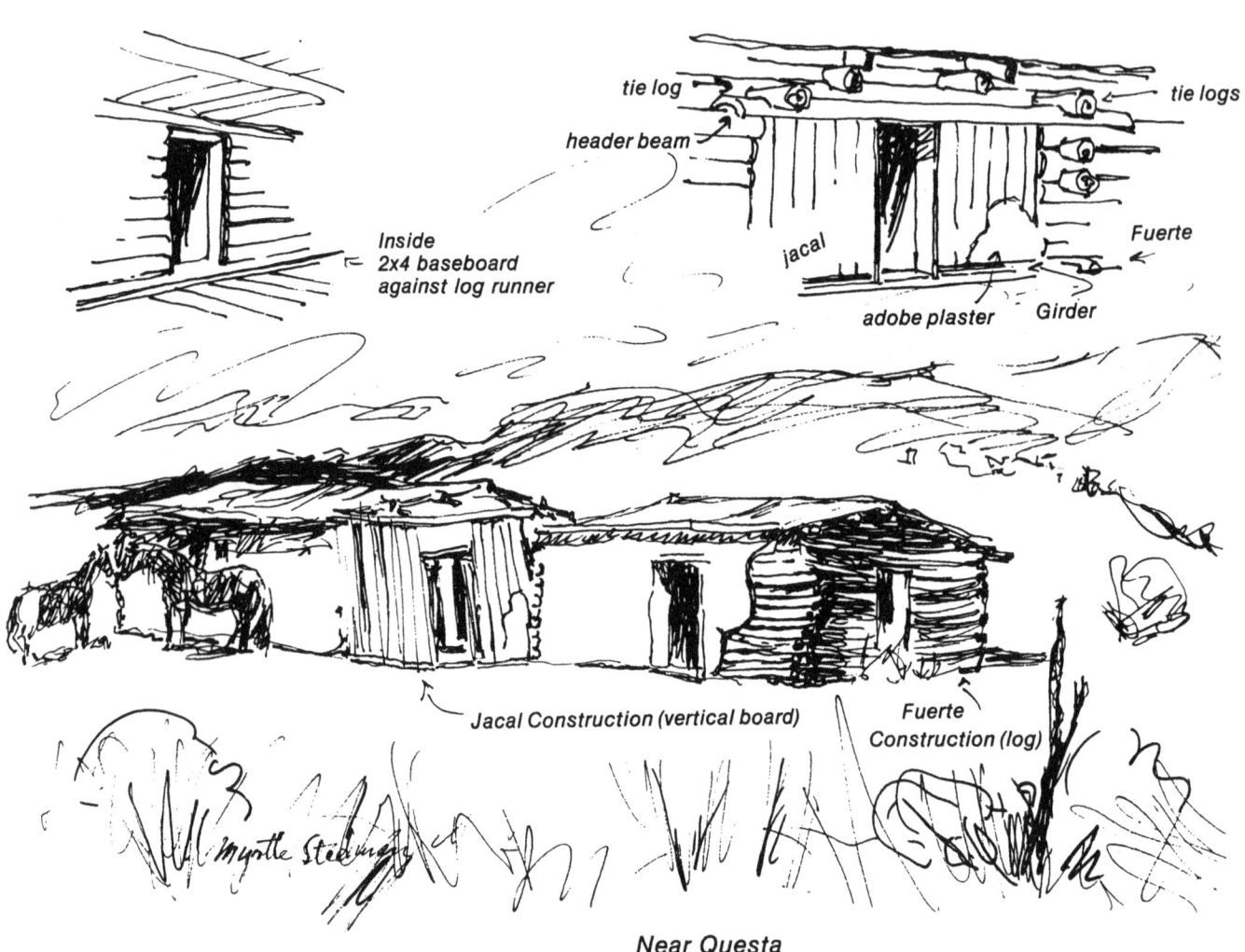

Near Questa
Abobe plastered jacal & Fuerte Ruin

Log Cabin. Hog-trough style with a Barrel Roof

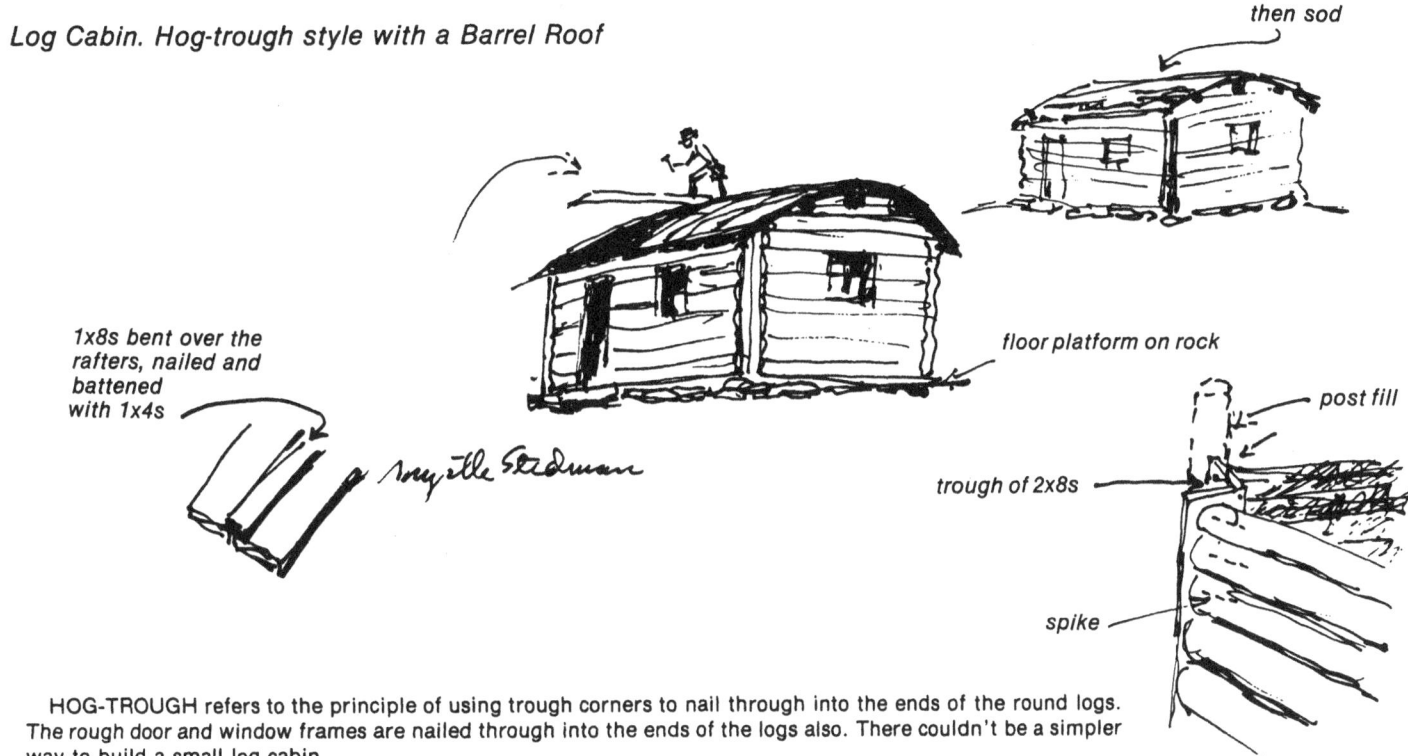

HOG-TROUGH refers to the principle of using trough corners to nail through into the ends of the round logs. The rough door and window frames are nailed through into the ends of the logs also. There couldn't be a simpler way to build a small log cabin.

The boy's cabin on the following page was moved about a mile from where it was originally built. Carpenter ants had hollowed out the inside of the huge center beam and it was about to collapse, along with the bottom logs, which were rotted.

The logs were numbered and given a wall identification, then the whole thing was dismantled and taken to a new location, where it was put up again on a new platform floor. Since their height was not needed, the rotted bottom logs were discarded and a new center beam and roof were put on.

A young boy's cabin in the woods,
a short distance from the main house.

Cottonwoods which were put in years ago as green fence posts along the Tesuque River.

Hay Stacks
 beside highway 10, above Walsenburg

In Cordova
Spanish American Hay Barns

The barns are log and the house adobe, but they are essentially the same style of architecture. Pitched roofs, to shed snow and rainfall, were first constructed of board and batten. After tin became commercially available, metal roofs were common when people could afford them. The pitched-roof barn might have been called *tasolera*, and the flat-roofed ones *fuertes*. The corner timbering would be a double-notched joint, either full or half.

In Truchas

The steep hillside on which these corrals and barns were built provided a very good example of land use. Heavy rainfall kept the footage space clean without much effort, and there were verdant fields below, plus miles for the water to become clean again before reaching the next village. On my last visit to this village, I observed most of these barns and corrals had been taken down and the lumber stacked for disposal.

Round log saddle-notch employed by both New Mexico cultures.

chinking between logs

not like this

In Truchas

An Equipment Shelter

This equipment shelter is built like the *portal* of the house on the next page and is on the same ranch. The adobe back wall of the shelter follows a roadway that passes the ranch.

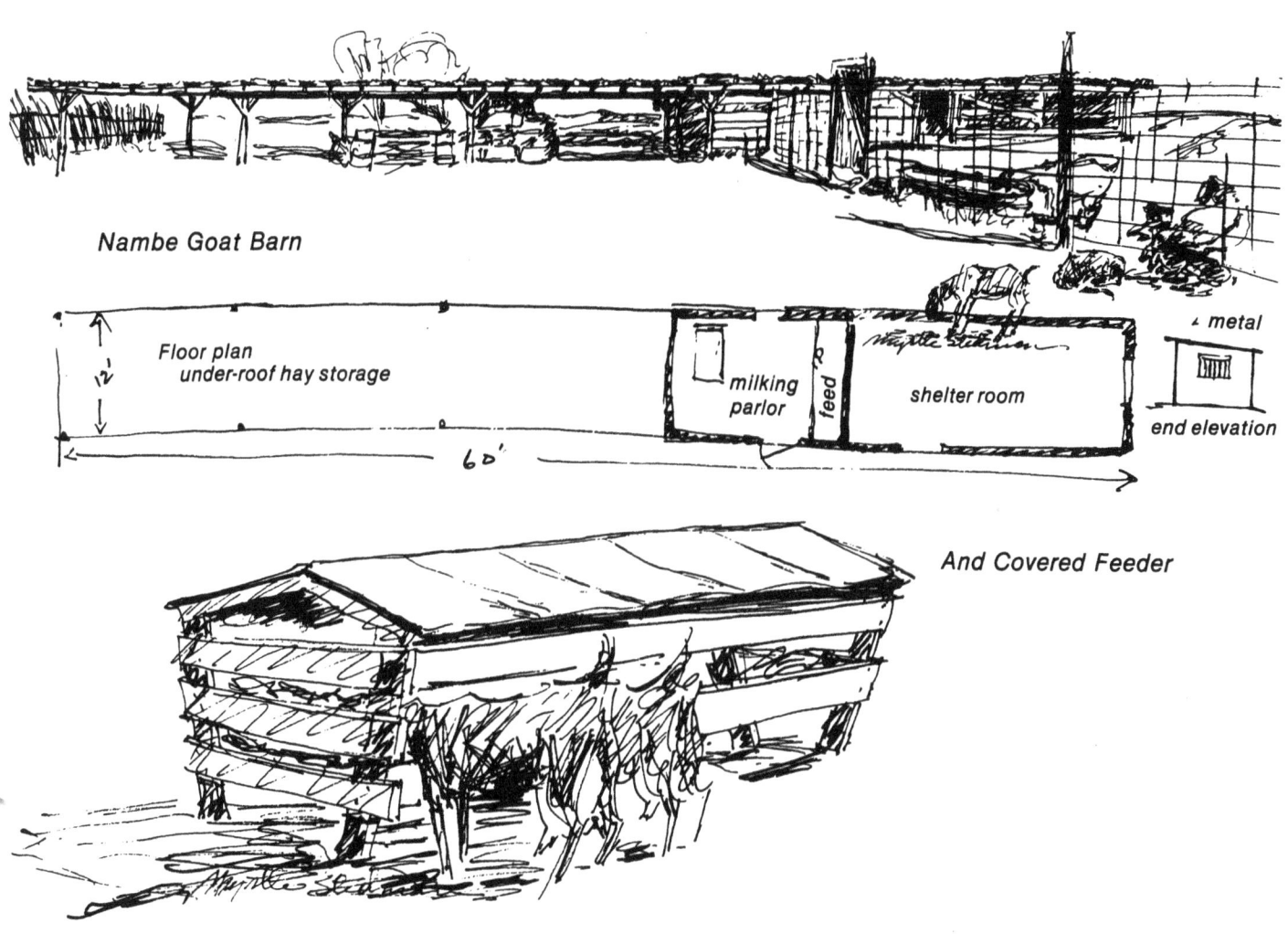

Nambe Goat Barn

And Covered Feeder

Pig Palace

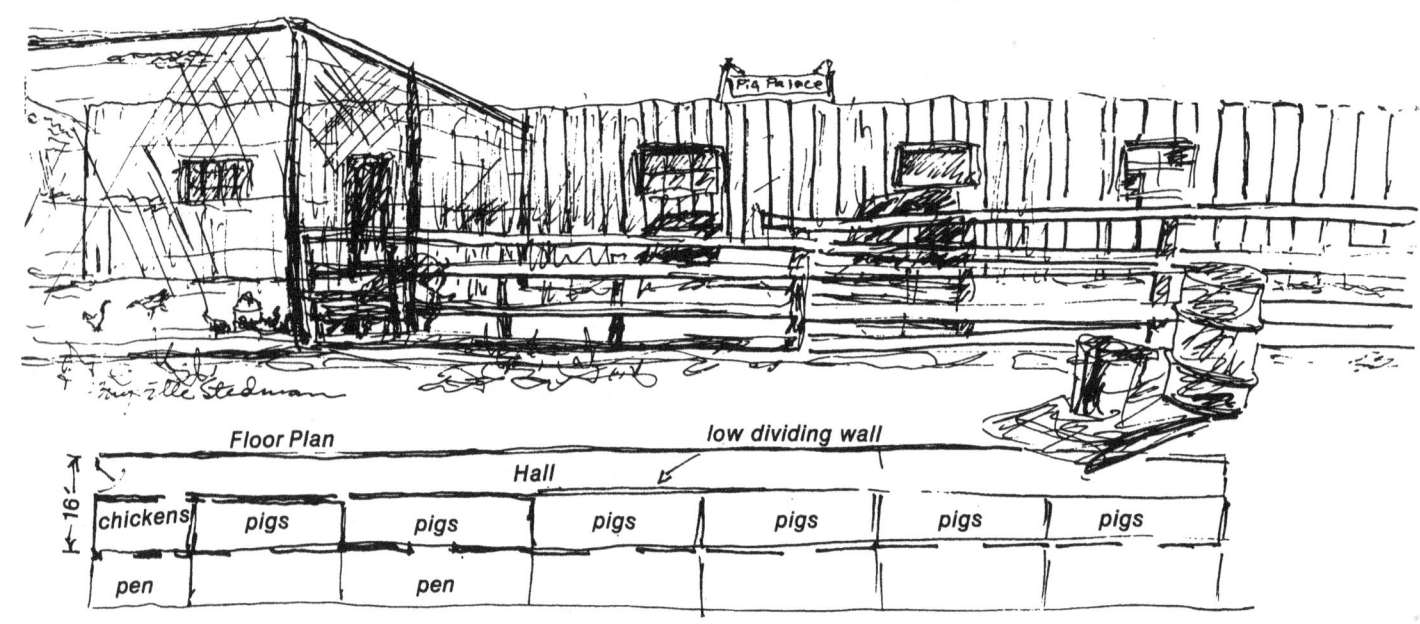

A long building with slab walls and flat slightly pitched roof.

50

Sheep Enclosures

I sketched the metal sheep barn on page 52 and thought to myself, "I won't need to see how it looks inside because it's probably just an open shelter," and drove on. Then I decided that I did want to see what was on the inside and, although I went back twice to where I thought it was, I couldn't find it.

The third time I was up that way but much farther north and, above Walsenburg on Highway 10, I found it. Just as I came to it, Mr. Corsentino was coming out of his barn. I told him who I was and what I was doing and asked him if I could see what was inside his barn (pg. 53). He said, "There's nothing in it." I said, "I mean I just want to see what's holding the roof up." "Well, all right," he said, "you're welcome," and helped me through the fence. "There's a billy goat in there, so I better go with you, because he may bother you." he continued.

There was also a ewe. Mr. Corsentino told me the barn had been a turkey barn before he decided to use it for sheep. He showed me where a refrigerated room used to be and then how he had converted the barn for sheep and hay storage.

He had a string of pens in which the ewes gave birth to their lambs in the spring. These were heated with heat lamps. In each pen there was a manger and a watering trough. The rest of the barn had pens where he could divide the sheep for shearing, inoculating, breeding, and the like. A large portion of the barn was given over to baled hay. He demonstrated to me how he could close in the entire place for winter.

I was very thankful to him and promised I would keep on the other side of the fence from the billy goat while making interior sketches. After he left, the two goats came and looked me over, but decided I wasn't a threat. The billy went a few feet from me and lay down while I sketched his portrait.

Metal Sheep Barn

At Cuyamungue

Covered Sheep Mangers

There is a walkway under a sheltering roof behind the mangers for carrying hay from the barn at the far right.

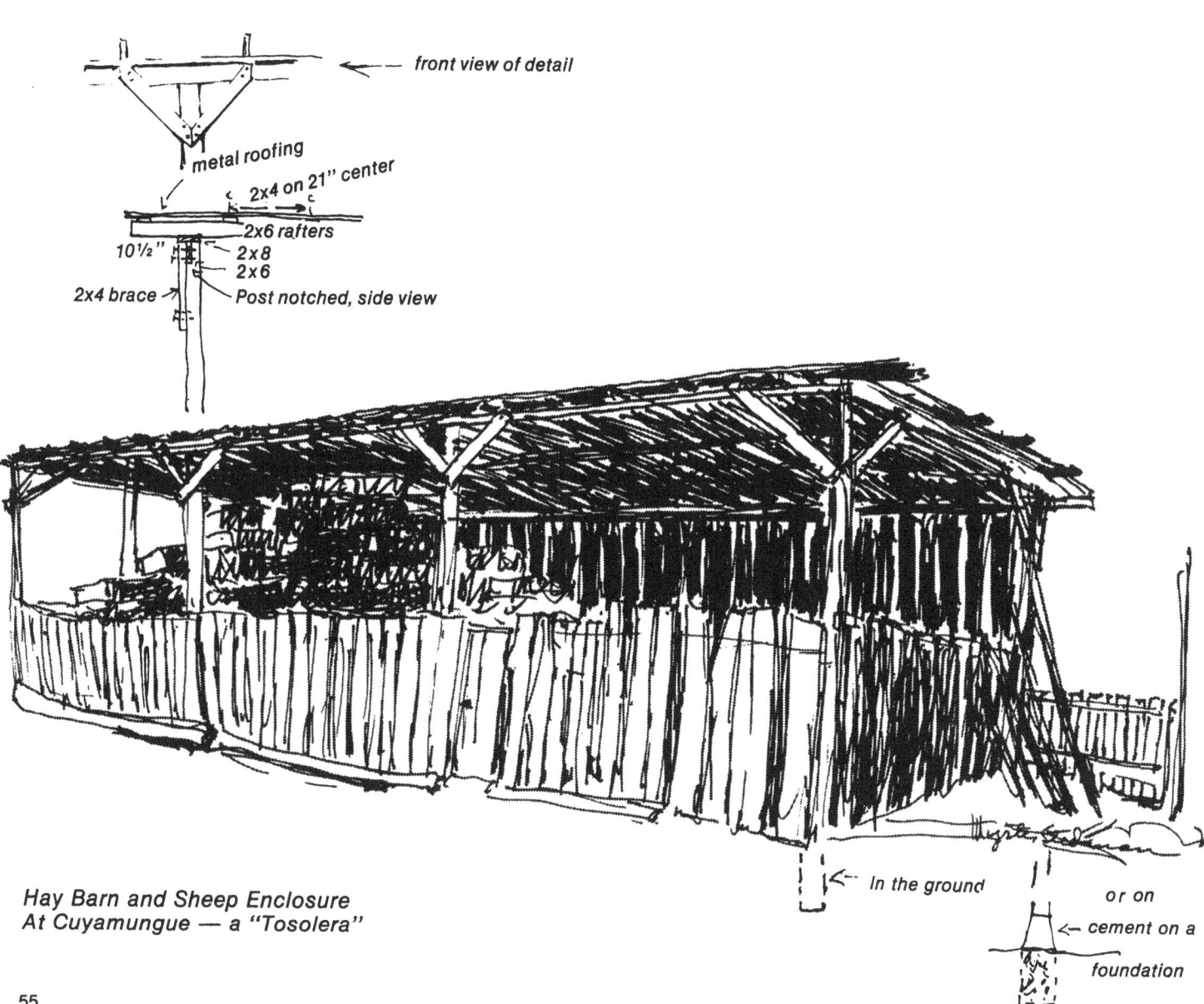

Hay Barn and Sheep Enclosure At Cuyamungue — a "Tosolera"

Sheep shelter, holding pen (a fold)

Sheepherder's Wagon

Dairy Barns

Feed lots and fences

At Placita

A very old square-cut log barn—but very much in use—with an open-ended hay loft. The hay barn beyond it and the corrals are of a later date. The cattle in the pasture look well-fed. This is in the high country where the roofs need to be pitched to shed the snow and heavy rainfall. The pitched roofs indicate a Spanish-American village.

A sign on the gate said PRIVATE PROPERTY, so I stayed in the car, though I would have like to talk with the two men who were busy at the barns.

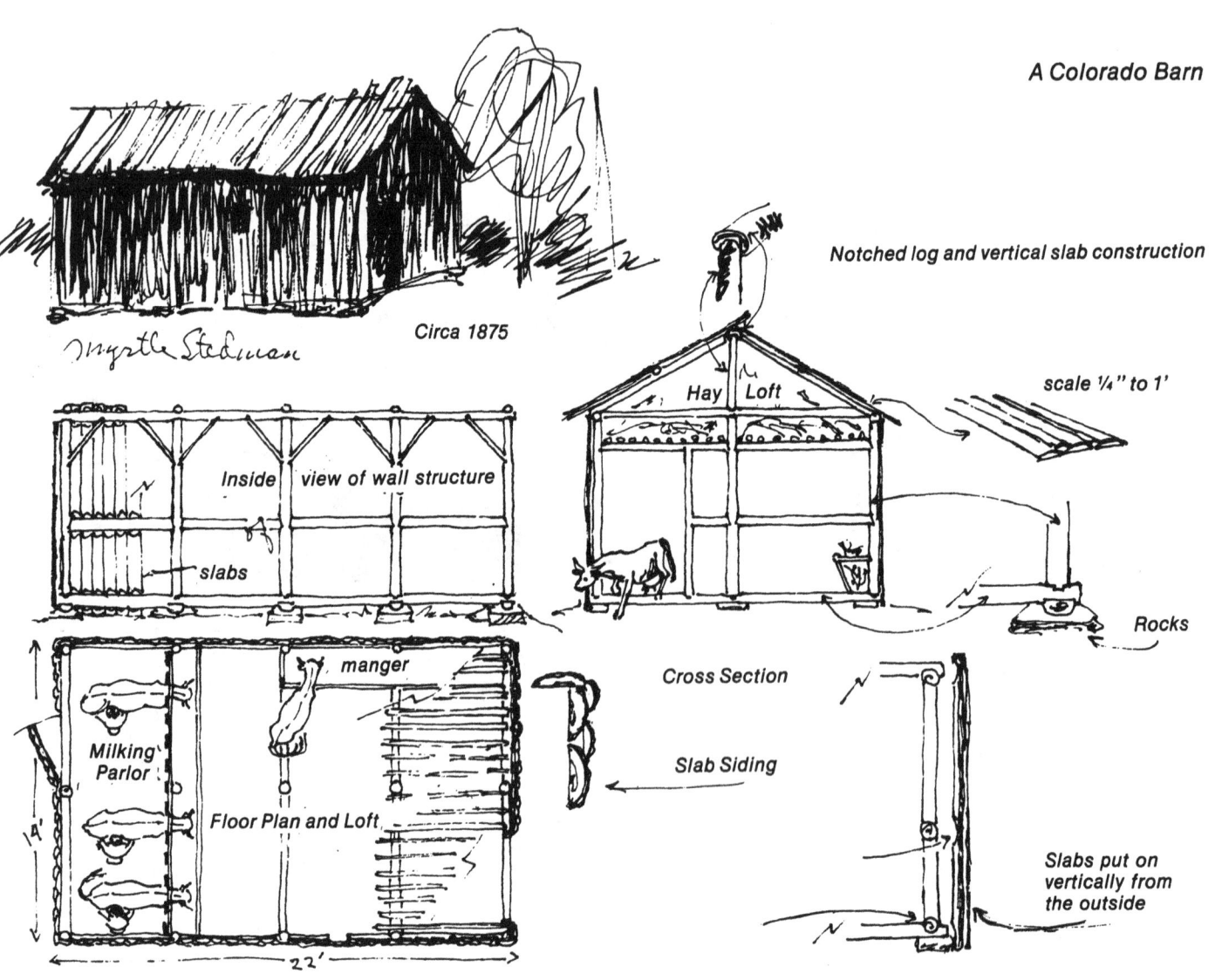

A Colorado Barn

At Llano

This barn is a beauty—two hay lofts with a loading platform in between, from which hay can be forked into either loft. Stables and a place for equipment below—board and batten roof with dormer vents—walls of squared log cabin style structure, except for the near end wall, which is wide vertical boards on a framework. This barn is pictured in *Pioneer America*, Vol. III, no. 2, July 1971, in an article by Charles F. Gritzner entitled "Log Housing in New Mexico," and is referred to as a "highly modified double-crib complex."

At Placita, log barn

The board-roofed area is probably very old. One can judge the size of the barn by the ladder on its roof—it probably has stables below, hay above, and the typical drive-through from front to back.

*Dairy Feed Lot
At Nambe*

The milking parlor, which I did not sketch, is a modern pumice block building adjoining this feed lot. *La tapeista*, the platform supported by upright posts upon which hay is stacked, is the most common type of farm structure in the Southwest (see "A Catalog of New Mexico Farm Building Terms" in *Landscape*, Winter 1952, Vol. I, no. 3, pp. 31-2). The larger barn for hay forage is called a *tasolera* in the same catalog.

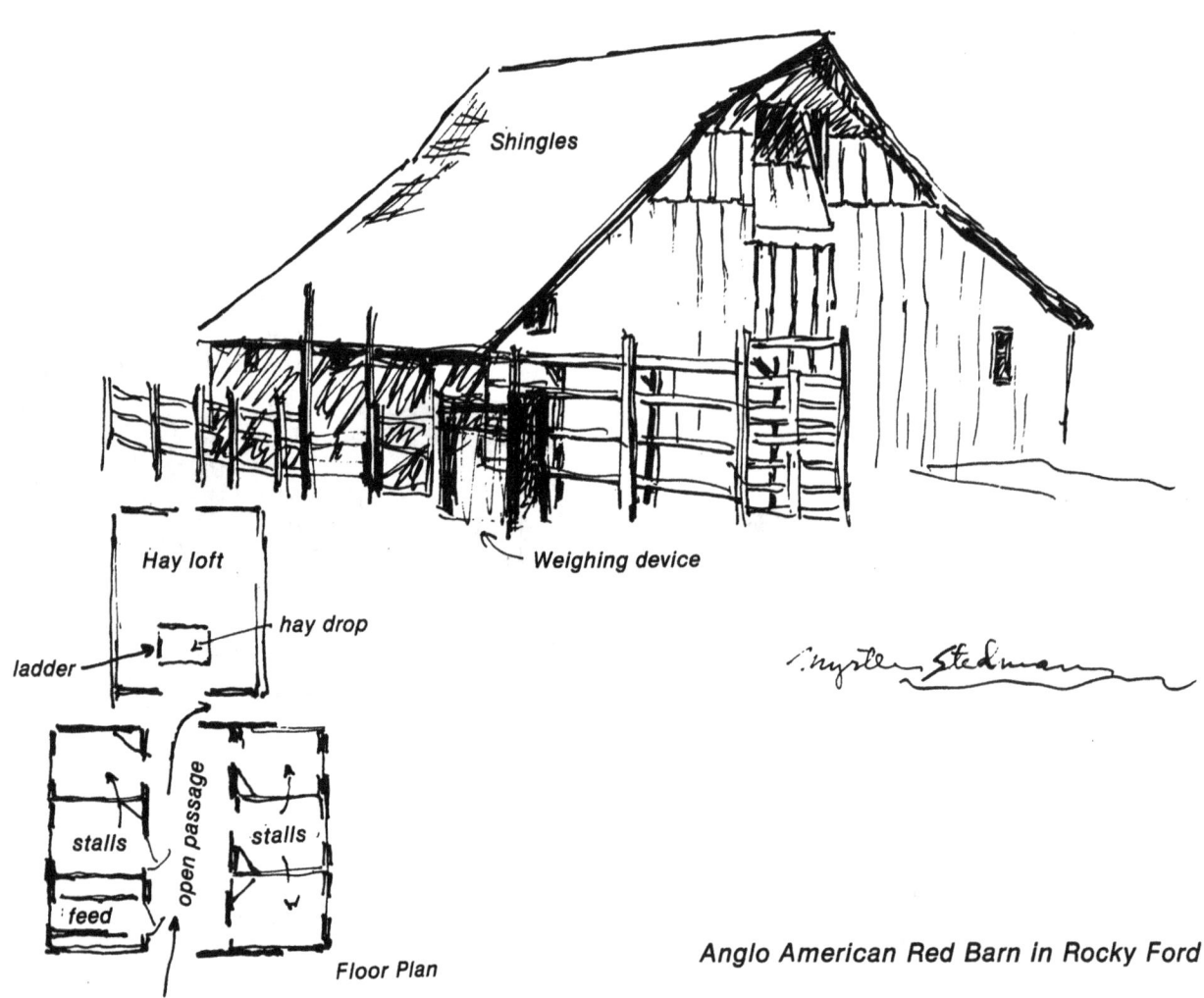

Anglo American Red Barn in Rocky Ford

Shelter, Corral and Loading Chute
At Taos Pueblo

Sambrel Roofs with a Dutch Look

Good wind deflection

Onion Storage Shed
Adobe walls

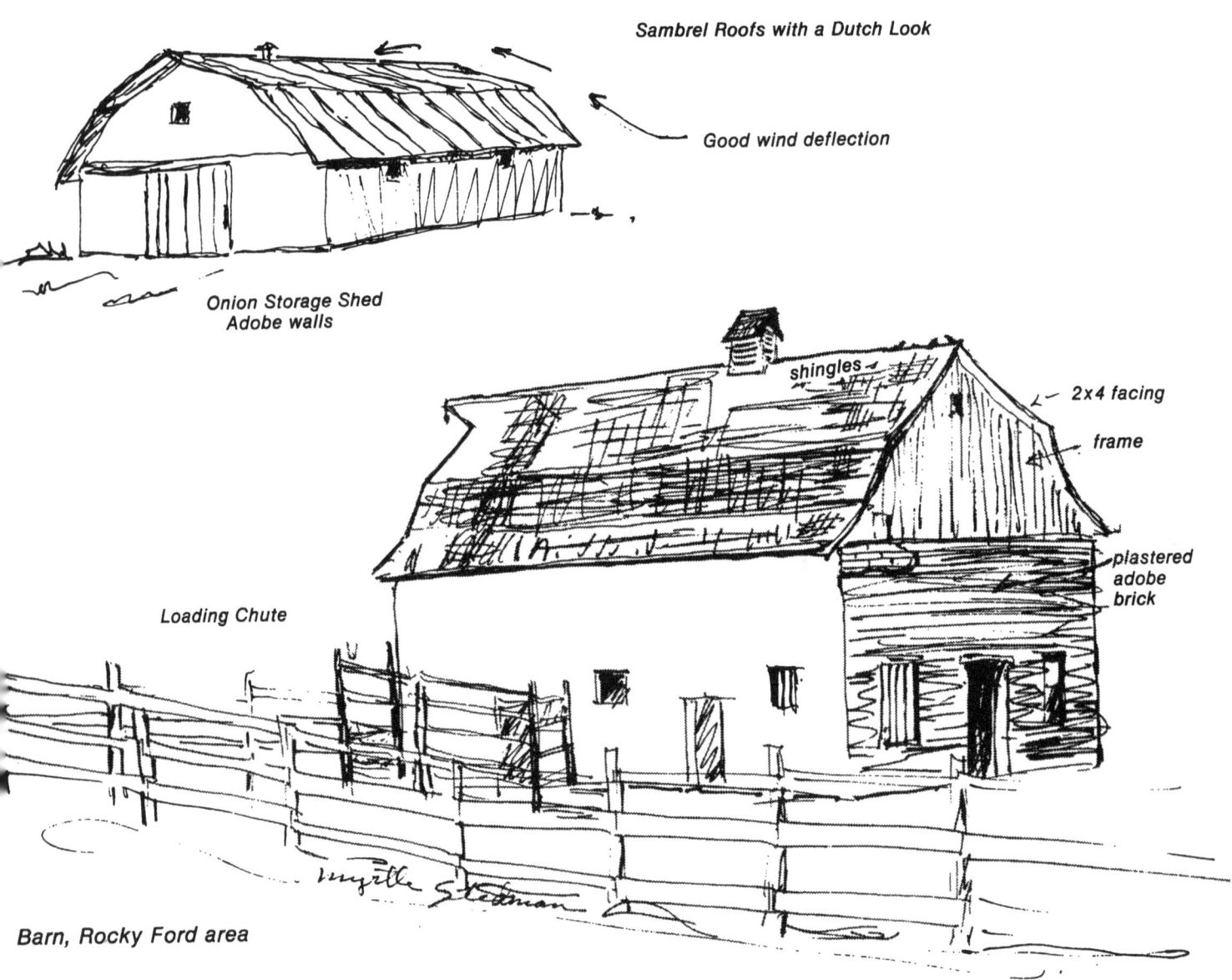

shingles
2x4 facing
frame
plastered adobe brick

Loading Chute

Barn, Rocky Ford area

AT Questa
Fuerte (adobe plastered log)
House built with same roof construction as bar on opposite page.

This all-frame barn is one of four built on a two-thousand acre cattle ranch—which could only support a hundred and ten cows. It lies on a flat, irrigated plain called a *llano*, where the slightest noise is absorbed in the vastness.

At Watrous

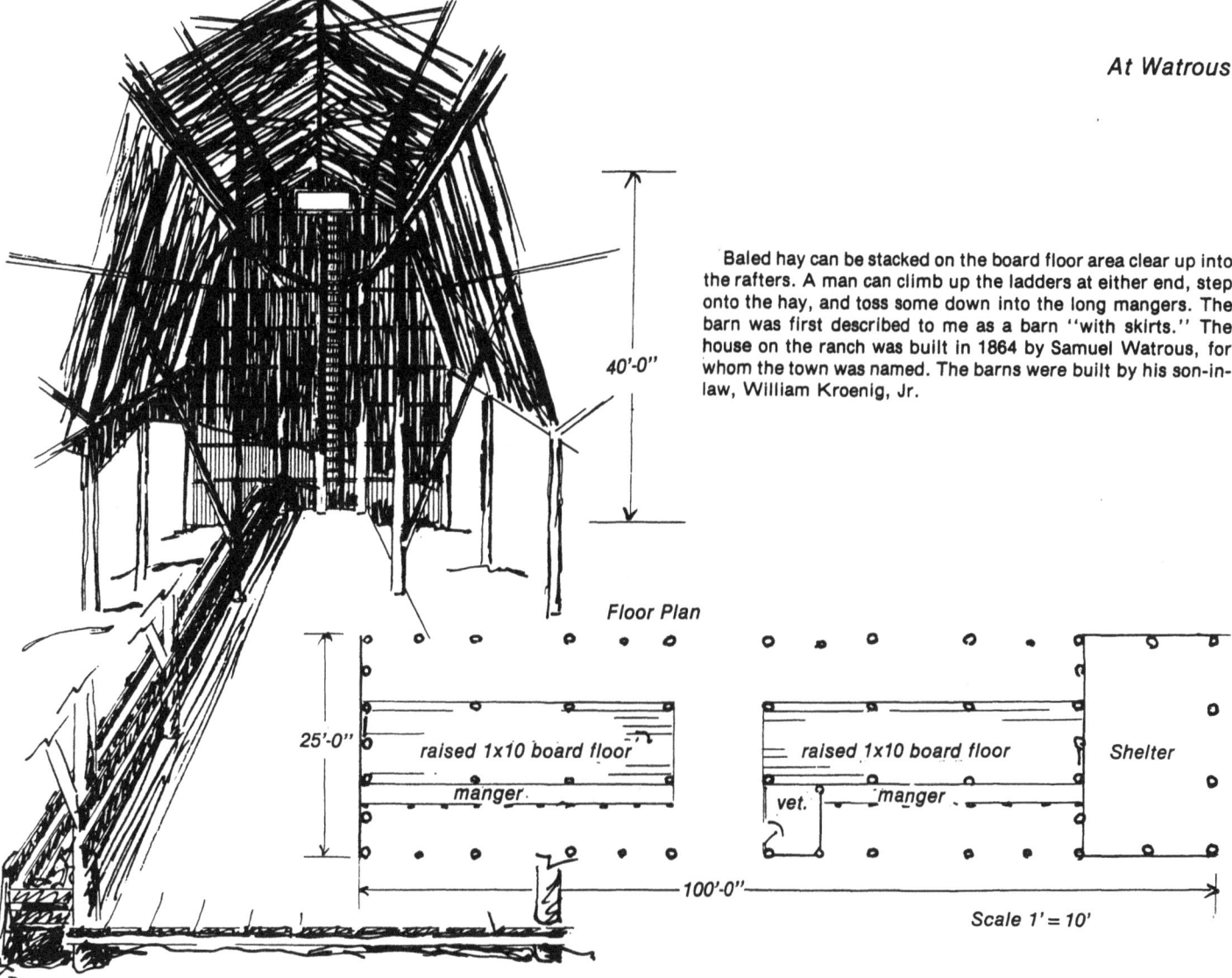

Baled hay can be stacked on the board floor area clear up into the rafters. A man can climb up the ladders at either end, step onto the hay, and toss some down into the long mangers. The barn was first described to me as a barn "with skirts." The house on the ranch was built in 1864 by Samuel Watrous, for whom the town was named. The barns were built by his son-in-law, William Kroenig, Jr.

Round Dairy Barn
  At Ojo Caliente Mineral Springs
    Built in the 1920s

The round barn was probably built by a wandering Shaker. It carries a Registered Cultural Property plaque (Site #503, State of New Mexico). I was glad to have the opportunity to spend two or three days making drawings and measurements of it to record in this book. It bears the mark of a master builder and perfectionist.

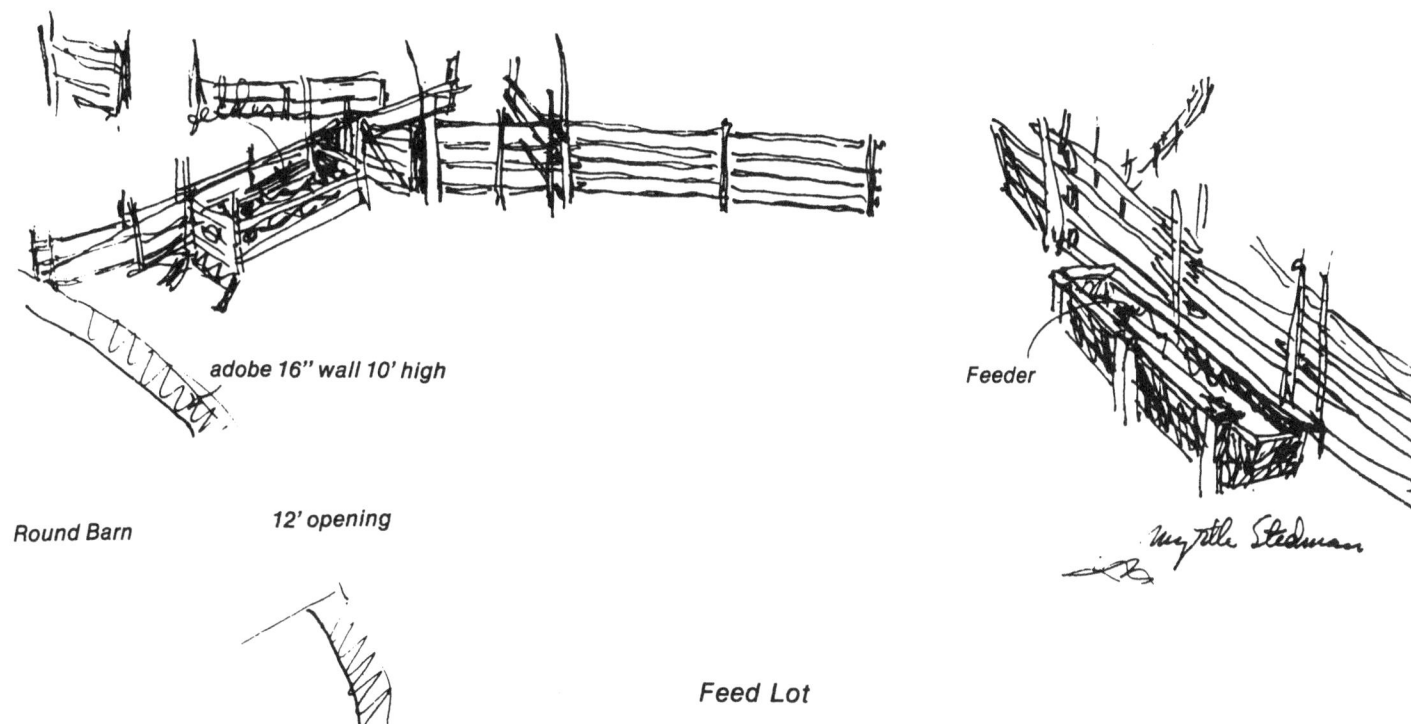

adobe 16" wall 10' high

Feeder

Round Barn 12' opening

Feed Lot

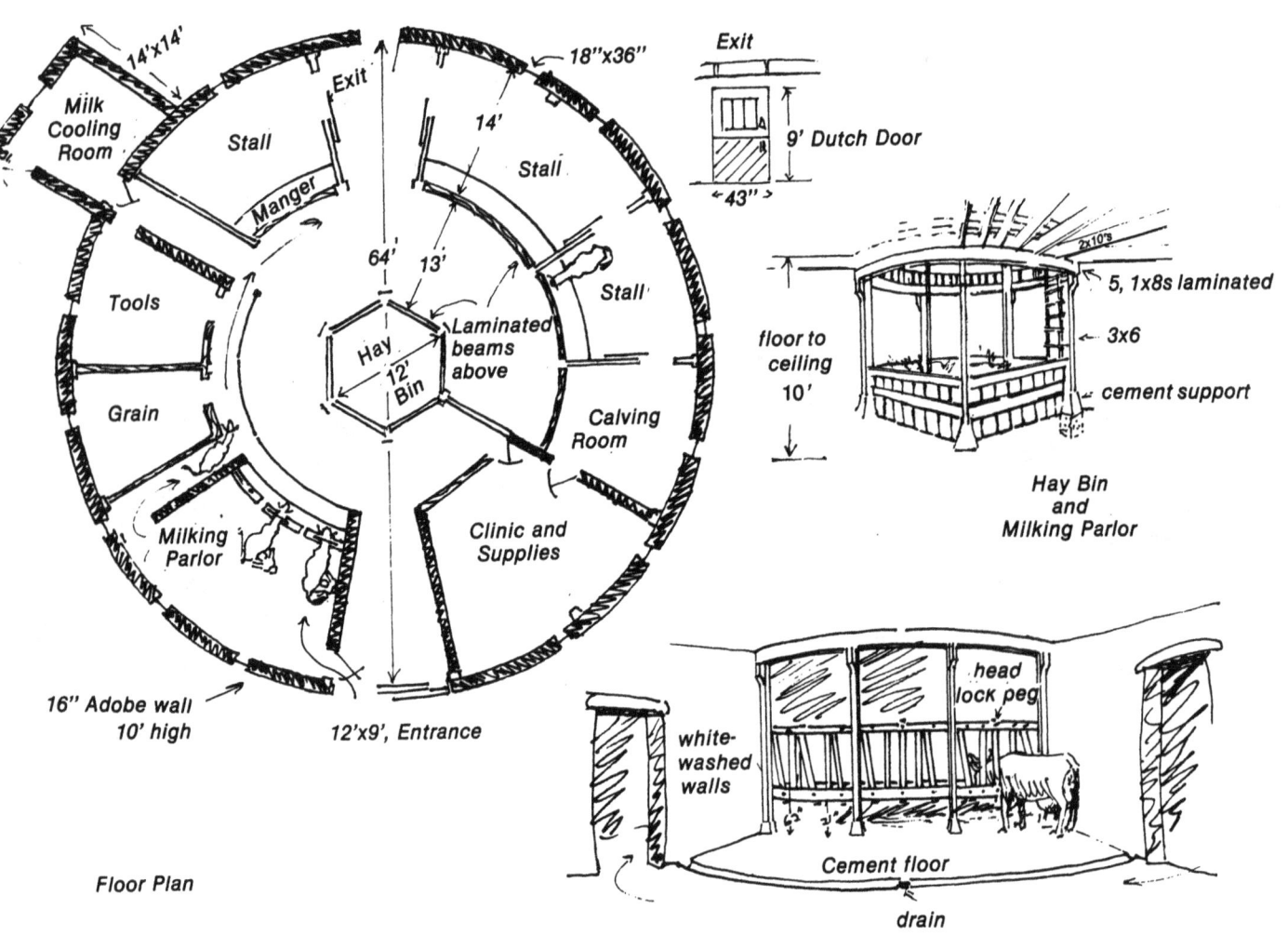

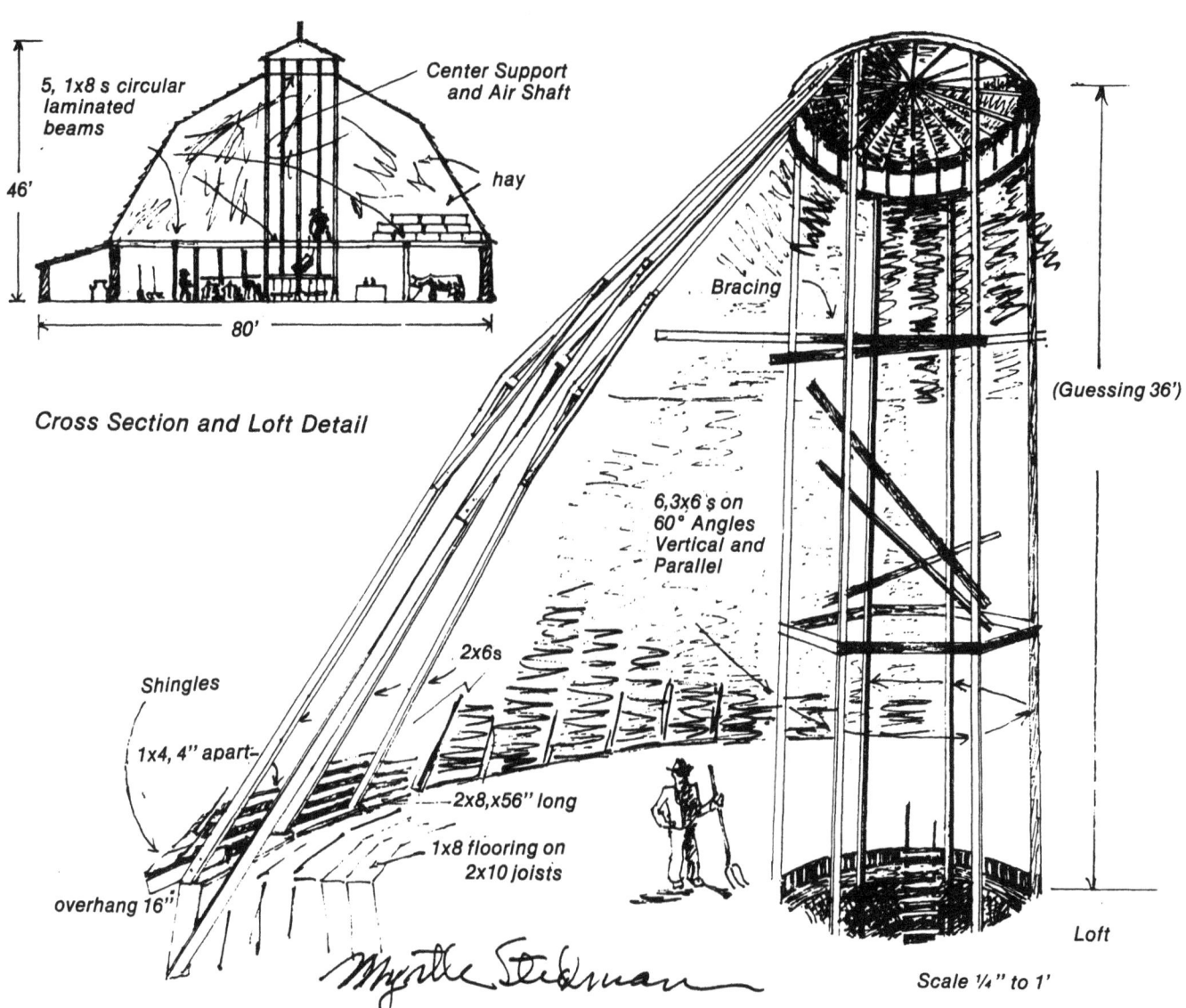

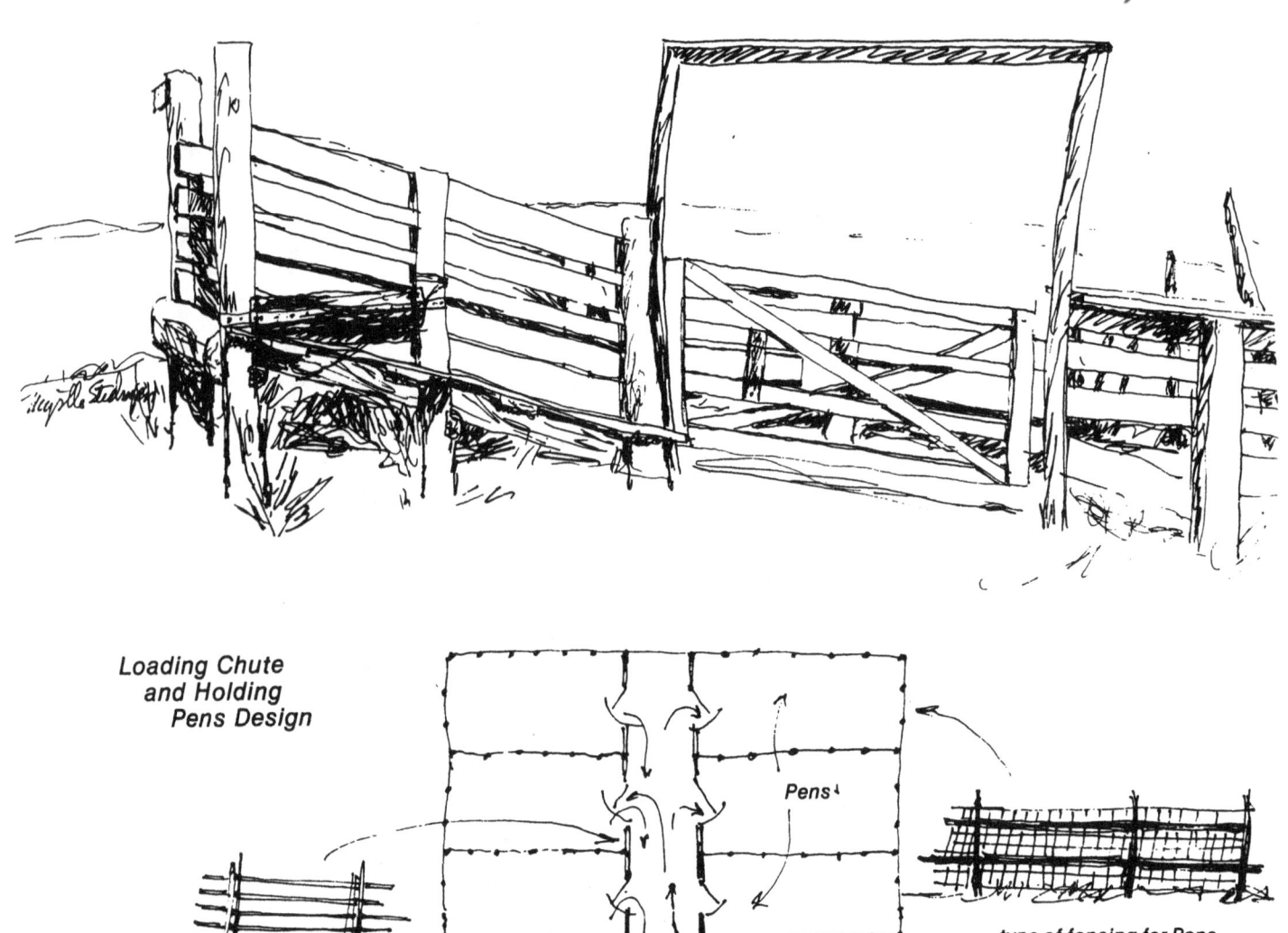

Loading Chute and Holding Pens Design

Loading Chute

Gate entrance

Pens

type of fencing for Pens

Farm Gates

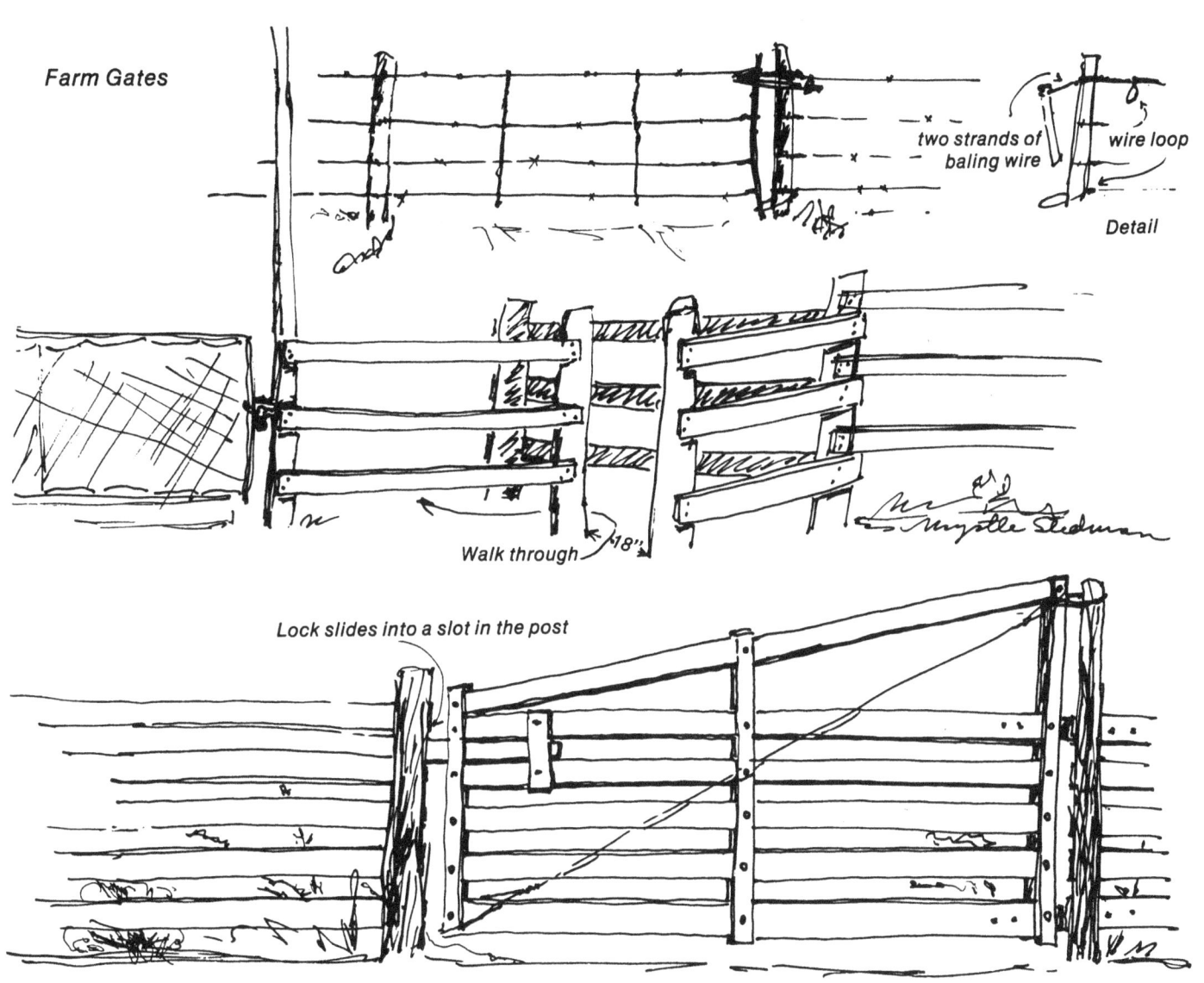

two strands of baling wire — wire loop

Detail

Walk through 18"

Lock slides into a slot in the post

Show Horses and Barns for them

Myrtle Stedman

76

On the Petchesky Quarter Horse Ranch — Santa Fe

Round Corral Diameter 36 feet
for lunging, breaking & training.

This barn has a *portal* and a corral off each of its four sides. The corrals, twenty-five by seventy-five feet, are calculated for two horses each. The *portals* plus a wall of the barn are said to be enough shelter from wind, rain and snow for the horses.

The inside of the barn measures twenty-five by fifty feet with a twelve-foot height to the wall plate; the ridge is a little higher and is left open at each end for ventilation. There is a twelve-by-fourteen foot tack room created by divider walls, and the rest of the place can hold fourteen hundred bales of hay.

The shelter which stands apart from the barn has a roof and a wind-break wrapped around on two sides. The wind-break is a specially coated fabric made by awning companies that make tarpaulins for transcontinental trucks. These are tied to the metal frames with baling wire. There is nothing the horse will chew on here but its food.

The Petcheskys call this room attached to their house a *horsepital*. They can look through a window of their home into this room to check on a sick horse or one that is about to foal without dressing and going out at night. It has a light and heat lamp, a dirt floor covered with straw bedding, a high ceiling, and is twelve by fourteen feet. The Petcheskys are very happy with it. It makes caring for their horses much safer and simpler for them.

This solar barn, gallery, and lounge represent the new look on the horizon. And, strangely enough, it exists in one of the oldest communities in New Mexico. I was in it on a winter day and was very comfortable. It is a beautifully built building.

Solar Barn

*Ground floor plan and
gallery above drawn
by Myrtle Stedman*

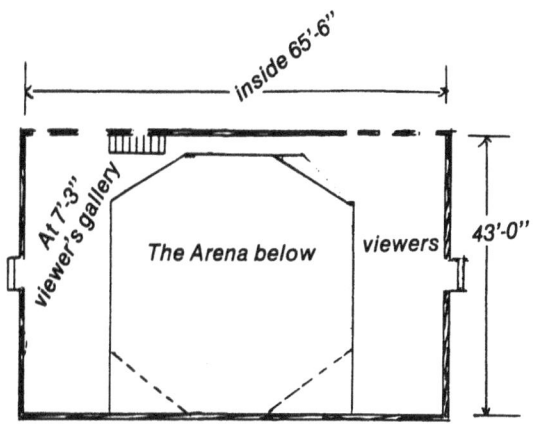

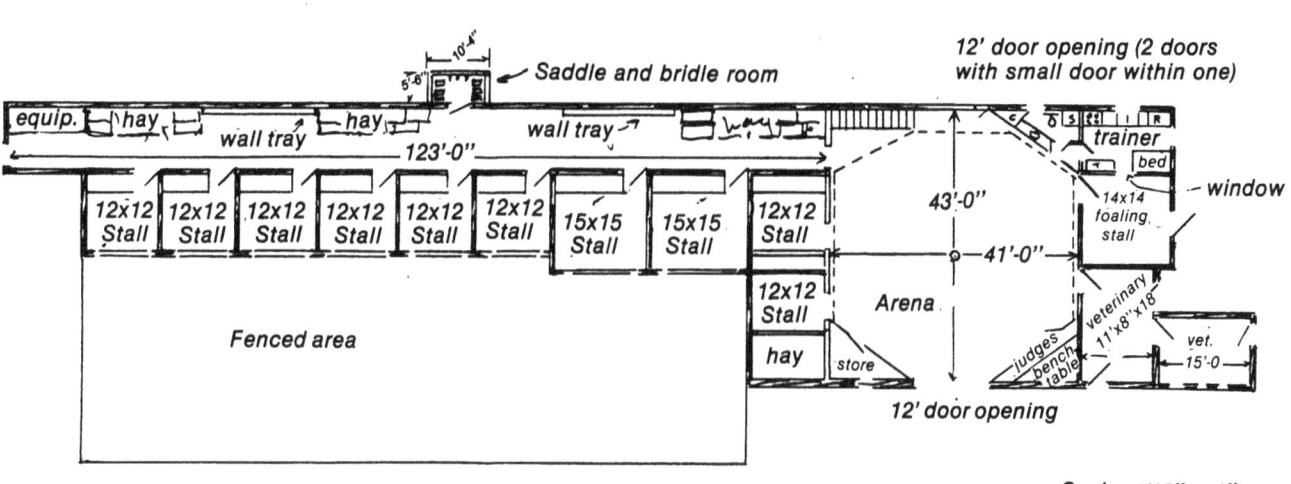

Scale 1/16" to 1"

**Barn & Caretaker's Place
Anglo American in Colorado**

You may not be able to do this these days, but this caretaker's residence over the stables guarantees a close watch on a sick horse or one about to foal. The stables are only used on a cold night or for holding horses for a short time. Many times a stable is the best place for taking care of a horse that would otherwise be running loose in the pastures. The siding on the barn is stained brown, and it is the rounded, first sawmill cut which gives the barn the appearance of a log cabin.

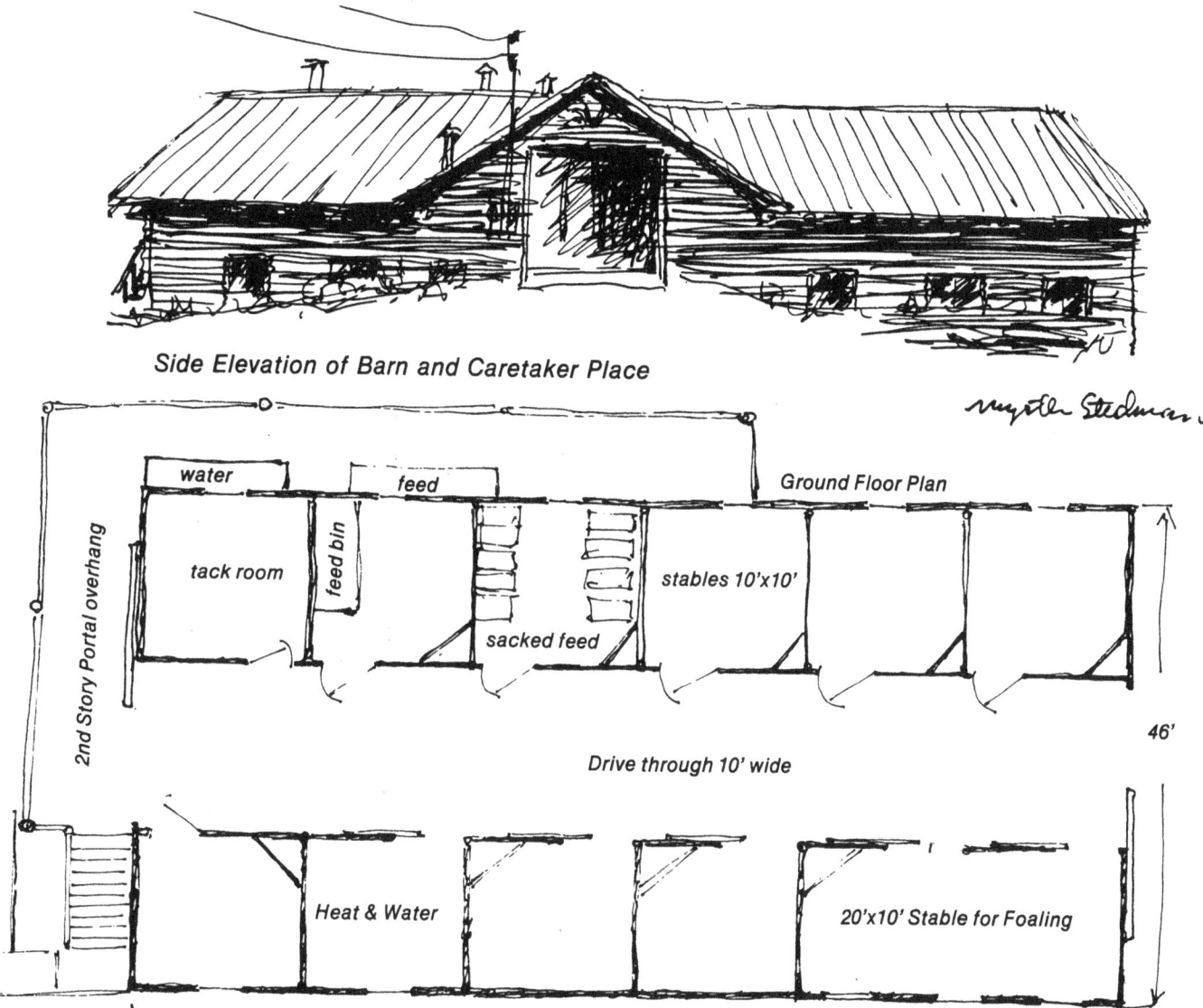

Side Elevation of Barn and Caretaker Place

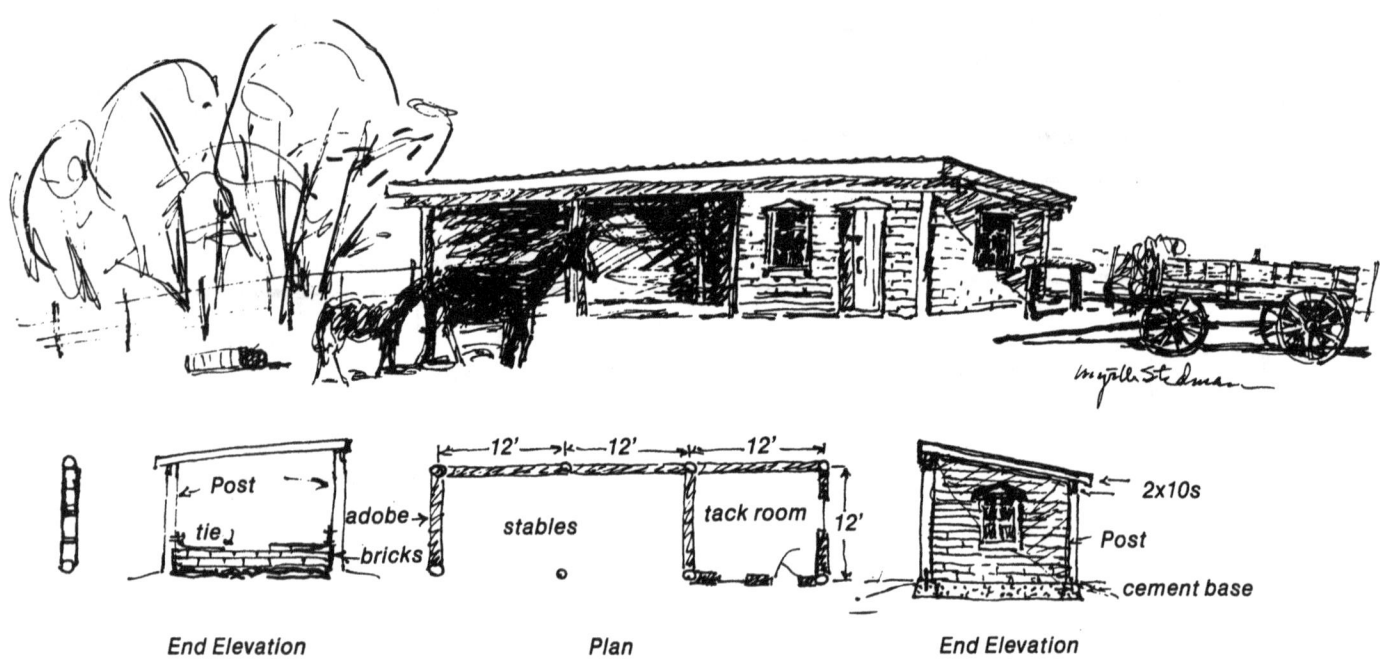

These stables and tack room began as a *loggia* (a roof atop posts) and, later, walls of semi-stabilized adobes were built in between the posts. The adobes were fitted to the posts and the walls were reinforced with two layers of Durowall which were attached to each post to bind all together. It was built in 1980 at a cost of $2,000.

I couldn't resist showing this sketch of a mare and two colts. A colt's legs at this early age are longer than its neck. It has to spread its legs to reach the bottom of a bucket. Two seconds after I made this sketch, one of the colts spread its legs, lost its balance, and did a somersault right over the bucket.

Albuquerque Fair Grounds Stables

BIBLIOGRAPHY

Arthur, Eric and Dudley Whitney. *The Barn: The Vanishing Landmark in North America*, Boston, New York Graphic Society, 1972.

Brooks, Eliot Wigginton. *The Foxfire Book*, Garden City, N.Y., Anchor/Doubleday, 1972.

Bunting, Baingridge, and Arthur Lazar. *Of Earth and Timbers Made: New Mexico Architecture*, Albuquerque, University of New Mexico Press, 1974.

"A Catalog of New Mexico Farm Buildings Terms," (no author given) *Landscape*, Vol. 1, No. 3, Winter 1952.

Gritzner, Charles F. "Hispanic Log Construction of New Mexico," *El Palacio*, Vol. 85, No. 4, Winter 1979/80.
"Log Housing in New Mexico."
Pioneer America, Vol. 3, No. 2, July 1971.

Horgan, Paul. *The Centuries of Santa Fe*, New York, E.P. Dutton, 1956.

Horn, Andrew. *Barns*, Berkeley, University of California Press, 1960.

Iowa, Jerome. *Ageless Adobe: History and Preservation in Southwestern Architecture*, Santa Fe, N.M., Sunstone Press, 1985.

Kirk, Ruth F. "Architecture: The Ancients," *New Mexico Magazine*, May 1941.

LaFarge, Oliver. *A Pictorial History of the American Indian*, New York, Crown Publishers, 1956.

Matthews, Truman, "Architecture with a Past," *New Mexico Magazine*, May 1952.

McCall, Ray; Chalom, Mark; and Quintin Wilson. *Principles of Solar Energy and Adobe Construction*, Abiquiu, N.M., Ghost Ranch Conference Center, 1977.

Momaday, N. Scott, and David Muench. *Colorado: Summer/Fall/Winter/Spring*, Chicago, New York, San Francisco, Rand McNally & Co., 1973.

Robinson, Ethel and Thomas. *The Houses in America*, New York, Viking Press, 1936.

Simmons, Marc. *New Mexico: A History*, New York, Norton, 1977.
Yesterday in Santa Fe, Cerrillos, N.M., San Marcos Press, 1969.

Sloane, Eric. *An Age of Barns*, New York, Ballantine, 1967.
American Barns and Covered Bridges, New York, Funk & Wagnalls, .

Stedman, Myrtle. *Adobe Remodeling*, Santa Fe, N.M., Sunstone Press, 1976.

Stedman, Myrtle. *Adobe Remodeling & Fireplaces*, Santa Fe, N.M., Sunstone Press, 1986.

Stedman, Myrtle & Wilfred Stedman. *Adobe Architecture*, Santa Fe, N.M., Sunstone Press, 2nd ed., *1987.*

U.S. Department of Agriculture. *Illustrated List of Farm Service Buildings and Equipment*, Beltsville, Md., U.S. Dept. of Agriculture, 1979.

Weslager, C.A. *The Log Cabin in America: From Pioneer Days to the Present*, New Brunswick, N.J., Rutgers University Press, 1969.

Myrtle Stedman, an artist, author, designer and builder, first learned about architecture from association with her father, E.B. Kelly, who designed and built homes and other buildings. Born in Charleston, Illinois, she grew up in Texas. She studied at the Houston Museum of Fine Arts.

A working partnership was established with her husband, Wilfred Stedman, in the fields of advertising, illustration and architecture. The Stedman Studio was first in Houston and in 1934 was relocated to Tesuque, New Mexico.

Following the death of Wilfred in 1950, Myrtle became known for her work in designing, building and remodeling adobe homes.

Her career as a fine artist has continued through the years and her paintings can be seen in several Southwestern galleries.

www.ingramcontent.com/pod-product-compliance
Lightning Source LLC
Chambersburg PA
CBHW080523110426

42742CB00017B/3218